Quick Java

"We'll be doing this next project in Java."

Unfortunately, you're a C++ programmer, or maybe a Python programmer. How are you going to get up to speed in a hurry? There are lots of Java books for beginners, telling you all about what a computer is and how it represents everything in bits. You don't need that. At the other extreme, there are thousand-page tomes that you aren't going to get through in a few days, if ever. You need something in-between.

This book is intended to fill that gap. It's written for the programmer who doesn't need to be taught how to program, just how to do it in Java—and who needs to get started in a hurry.

Java is covered from the inside out. First, all the things that go inside a class, most of which are practically identical to C++. After that, all the various and complicated kinds of classes and interfaces and how they relate to each other in large-scale programs.

Testing is essential, so (unlike most Java books) JUnit is covered in detail. Then, in case you need to go in that direction, some functional programming, a little about parallel programming, and more than enough to get you started in building GUIs (graphical user interfaces) and doing animation.

There's a lot in this little book and, despite my best efforts, you won't learn Java in a weekend. But it should be a good start.

FEATURES

- Circular approach allows very fast entry into Java
- Full description of JUnit testing
- Summary of functional programming in Java
- Introduction to synchronization and parallel processing
- Extensive description of building GUIs

Quick Java

David Matuszek

CRC Press
Taylor & Francis Group
Boca Raton London New York

CRC Press is an imprint of the
Taylor & Francis Group, an **informa** business

A CHAPMAN & HALL BOOK

Designed cover image: David Matuszek

First edition published 2024
by CRC Press
2385 NW Executive Center Drive, Suite 320, Boca Raton FL 33431

and by CRC Press
4 Park Square, Milton Park, Abingdon, Oxon, OX14 4RN

CRC Press is an imprint of Taylor & Francis Group, LLC

© 2024 David Matuszek

Library of Congress Cataloging-in-Publication Data
Names: Matuszek, David L., author.
Title: Quick Java / David Matuszek.
Description: First edition. | Boca Raton : CRC Press, 2024. | Series: Quick programming | Includes bibliographical references and index.
Identifiers: LCCN 2023011142 (print) | LCCN 2023011143 (ebook) | ISBN 9781032502779 (paperback) | ISBN 9781032515830 (hardback) | ISBN 9781003402947 (ebook)
Subjects: LCSH: Java (Computer program language)
Classification: LCC QA76.73.J38 M35257 2024 (print) | LCC QA76.73.J38 (ebook) | DDC 005.13/3--dc23/eng/20230609
LC record available at https://lccn.loc.gov/2023011142
LC ebook record available at https://lccn.loc.gov/2023011143

ISBN: 978-1-032-51583-0 (hbk)
ISBN: 978-1-032-50277-9 (pbk)
ISBN: 978-1-003-40294-7 (ebk)

DOI: 10.1201/9781003402947

Typeset in Minion
by MPS Limited, Dehradun

To all my students
past, present, and future

Contents

Author

I'M DAVID MATUSZEK, known to most of my students as "Dr. Dave." I wrote my first program on punched cards in 1963 and immediately got hooked.

I taught my first computer classes in 1970 as a graduate student in computer science at the University of Texas in Austin. I eventually got my PhD from there, and I've been teaching ever since. Admittedly, I spent over a dozen years in industry, but even then I taught as an adjunct at Villanova University.

I finally escaped from industry and joined the Villanova faculty full-time for a few years, then I moved to the University of Pennsylvania, where I directed a Master's in Computer and Information Technology (MCIT) program for students entering computer science from another discipline. Throughout my career, my main interests have been in artificial intelligence (AI) and programming languages. I've used a *lot* of programming languages.

I retired in 2017, but I can't stop teaching, so I'm writing a series of "quick start" books on programming and programming languages. I've also written three science fiction novels—*Ice Jockey*, *All True Value*, and *A Prophet in Paradise*—and I expect to write more. Check them out!

And, hey, if you're a former student of mine, drop me a note. I'd love to hear from you at david.matuszek@gmail.com.

Preface

I F YOU ARE AN EXPERIENCED PROGRAMMER, this book is your guide to getting up to speed in Java in a hurry. Not just the language, but also the basics of unit testing, graphical user interfaces, threads, animation, and functional programming.

If you are coming from one of the C languages, you will find most of the statement types familiar. These are clearly designated, so you can just skim over that material.

If you are coming from C++, you will find the object-oriented concepts are very similar, but the terminology is different.

If you are coming from another language, such as Python, there is very little you can skip. Sorry.

Let's get started!

Versions

THIS BOOK IS ABOUT **Java 8** and **Java 17**. Why those two?

Java 8 is the last version that is free for commercial use. If you are programming for Android, Java 8 (also known as version 1.8) is the last version you can use. For these reasons, additions to Java after version 8 will be noted as such.

As this book is being written, the current version is 17. A new version is released every six months, so when you buy this book, the latest version number is probably higher. This should not be a concern, because Java "never throws anything away." Newer versions do not invalidate older versions, and the language changes gradually. In fact, Java 17 is an *LTS* (*Long Term Support*) version, along with versions 8 and 11.

If you are uncertain which version of Java you have, you can execute this from the command line:

```
java -version
```

or execute the following `println` statement from within a running Java program:

```
System.out.println(System.getProperty("java.version"));
```

Since Java 9, you can also run `jshell` from the command line. This program lets you execute Java statements (such as the above print statement) one at a time. This is no way to write a program, but it's handy for trying things out.

If you have yet to download Java, it comes in two main varieties: the *JRE* (*Java Runtime Environment*) is used to run existing programs, and the *JDK* (*Java Development Kit*), which is used to create and run programs (the JDK contains the JRE). Since you are reading this book, you almost certainly want the JDK.

You can get the Java SE (Standard Edition) JDK from https://www.oracle.com/java/technologies/downloads/.

Java 9 and beyond are (currently) free for personal use, but commercial users should obtain a license from the Oracle Corporation.

CHAPTER 1

A Lightning Tour of Java

T HIS BOOK IS DESIGNED TO GET the experienced programmer in some other language to start programming in Java as quickly as possible. Consequently, this first chapter is very condensed and takes a great deal for granted; you do not have to understand or remember everything in the first reading. Later chapters will cover the same material more slowly and in greater detail.

> **Note:** Java is verbose, and code lines are often 80 to 100 characters long. Such lines have been split into more but shorter lines in an attempt to improve readability.

1.1 PROJECTS

A program, or *project*, consists of one or more *packages*. A *package* is a directory or folder that contains Java files.

Java files contain *classes*, usually one class per file. A class describes a new type of *object*, and bundles together the object's *fields* (its data) and its *methods*. A class has one or more *constructors* to create new objects of that type.

DOI: 10.1201/9781003402947-1

A method is like a function, except that a method belongs to an object, and (normally) works with the fields of that object. A method may contain **declarations** of variables and will contain executable statements.

To summarize, here is how a project is organized:

- packages (directories) of files
  - classes (generally one per file); each class contains:
    - fields (the data)
    - constructors, containing declarations and statements
    - methods, containing declarations and statements

In addition to the above, packages in Java 9 and later can be organized into even larger units, called **modules**. This is appropriate for programs with large numbers of packages. The JDK (Java Development Kit) is huge, consisting of about a hundred modules, hundreds of packages, and thousands of classes. The single module relevant to this book is java.base.

Modules will be discussed briefly in section 5.3.9.

1.2 FIRST GLIMPSE: THE CIRCLE CLASS

The following program demonstrates the overall structure of a Java program and provides an initial glimpse into what a Java program looks like.

```java
package examples.shapes;

public class Circle {
    private int radius;

    public Circle(int r) {
        radius = r;
    }

    public double area() {
        return Math.PI * Math.pow(radius, 2);
    }
}
```

The package declaration says that this code is in a folder (directory) named shapes which is in a folder (directory) named examples. If any import declarations were needed (none are), they would immediately follow this line.

The code defines a public class named Circle. The word public means that the class can be used by any code throughout the program. Because Circle is a public class, it must be on a file named Circle.java; this allows other code to find it.

The Circle class has one integer *instance variable* named radius. Every new Circle object that is created will have its own radius, and because radius is marked private, it cannot be seen outside this class.

Next is a constructor. It is recognizable as a constructor because it has the exact same name (Circle) as the class in which it occurs. It takes an integer parameter r, saves the value of r in its own instance variable radius, and returns a newly created Circle object. It does not use a return statement.

Finally, there is a method area that takes no parameters. It computes and returns the area of this circle.

Now that we have a Circle class, let's use it.

```
package examples.shapes;

public class CircleApp {

    public static void main(String[] args) {
        int size = 10;
        Circle c = new Circle(size);
        double area = c.area();
        System.out.printf(
            "The area of a circle " +
            "with radius %d is %7.2f",
            size, area);
    }
}
```

This class, CircleApp, happens to be in the same directory as the Circle class.

`CircleApp` does not have an explicit constructor (it has an implicit one, but ignore that for now). It does have a `main` method, which is the starting point for the program. For complex reasons, the `main` method is always defined as `public static void main(String[] args)`—just memorize this for now; understanding will come later.

The `main` method then:

- Declares a local variable `size` as an integer and gives it a value of 10.

- Declares another local variable `c` of type `Circle` and uses the keyword `new` to call the `Circle` constructor. It gets back a newly created `Circle` object and assigns it to `c`.

- Asks `c` for its `area`, and assigns the result to the double (floating point) variable `area`.

- Prints the result:

  `The area of a circle with radius 10 is 314.16`

1.3 DATA

Every data value in Java is either a *primitive* or an *object*. There are eight kinds of primitives, most of them numeric types. Objects are defined by *classes*, and each class defines a new type of object.

The four most important types of primitive are: `int` (integers, or whole numbers), `double` (numbers containing a decimal point), `boolean` (the values `true` and `false`), and `char` (individual characters).

Two important types of object are *strings* and *arrays*. Strings are objects defined by the `String` class, while arrays are defined using a more traditional syntax (but they are still objects.)

An obvious distinction between primitives and objects is that primitives have *operations*: `3 * n`, `big && round`, and so on, while objects have *methods*. (Exception: The + operator can be used to *concatenate* ("add") strings.)

Terminology: You don't "call" a method. Instead, you "send a message to an object," where the "message" consists of the method name and its parameters.

To send a message to an object, use **dot notation** like this: **object.method** (**parameters**). For example, firstName.charAt(0).

Literal strings are enclosed in double quotes: "Hello". Character literals are written in single quotes: 'a'.

All variables must be **declared** before use; this specifies their type. They can also be **defined**, or given an initial value.

```
int count;      // declaration
count = 0;      // definition
int count = 0; // declaration + definition
```

All the values in an array must be of the same type. The type of the array is written as the type of the elements, followed by empty brackets. For example, int[] denotes an array of integers. The length of an array is not part of the declaration; it is part of a definition.

```
int[] numbers = new int[100];
```

Arrays are **zero-based**. The first element in the above numbers array is numbers [0], and the last element is numbers [99]. The length of this array, 100, is given by numbers.length.

The values in a newly-declared array will all be zero (for numeric arrays), false (for boolean arrays), or null (for arrays of objects). Because characters are treated as numeric values, the values in an array of char will be the character "NUL" whose code is zero.

1.4 OPERATORS

Java has the usual arithmetic operators: + (add), - (subtract, or unary minus), * (multiply), / (divide), and % (remainder, or modulus). The multiplicative operators *, /, and % are done before the additive operators + and -. Operations of the same precedence are done left to right.

There is no exponentiation operator. Exponentiation is done by calling the pow method in the Math module: Math.pow(r, 2).

Arithmetic expressions using only integers result in an integer result. If the expression involves a double, the result will be a double.

Java has the boolean operators && (and), || (or), and ! (not). The comparison operators <, <=, == (equals), != (not equal), >, and >= all result in booleans. Booleans are not numbers, and you cannot use a number where a boolean is expected.

See section 3.2.5 for more detailed information on operators.

1.5 PROGRAM STRUCTURE

A Java program consists of one or more ***classes***. Each class is typically in a file of its own, named after the class but with the.java extension. If a class is named Example, it should be in a file named Example.java.

A Java file may contain a package declaration, which names the folder that the file is in, and some import declarations, to give the current class access to classes in other packages. (Classes in the same package don't need to be explicitly imported.) The code for the class follows these initial declarations.

```
package teamMaker;
import java.util.HashSet;
```

Note: An asterisk ("star") may be used to import all the classes in a package, for example, import java.util.*;.

A ***class*** is a recipe, or blueprint, for making objects. Classes contain declarations, constructors, and methods.

```
public class ClassName {
    declarations
    constructors
    methods
}
```

Classes marked public are available everywhere throughout the program.

A *declaration* consists of a type, a name, an optional equals sign, and a value, and ends with a semicolon. It may be marked as public or private, and in addition, it may be preceded by the word static.

```
public static double Avogadro = 6.0221409e+23;
```

If a variable is marked with static, there is only one of it, it belongs to the class itself, and all objects of that class share this one variable. Otherwise, it is an *instance variable* (also called a *field*), and every object has a separate copy of that variable.

A *constructor* is used to create new objects whose type is *ClassName*.

ClassName(parameters) {
  declarations
  statements
}

A constructor is called with new *ClassName(arguments)*. It *always* returns a newly created object; a return statement is unnecessary, and if used, it must be a "bare" return statement, not supplying a value. A constructor typically does little more than assign values to the instance variables of the new object.

A *method* is a callable chunk of code. It is like a function, except that it belongs to an object (or to a class). The basic structure of a method is

returnType methodName(parameters) {
  declarations
  statements
}

The *returnType* may be any primitive or object type, or the keyword void. If the *returnType* is void, the method will return when a return; statement is executed, or when the end of the method is reached. But if the method is to return a value, it must terminate with a return *expression*;

statement, where **expression** results in a value that can be put in a variable of type **returnType**.

To send a message to an object (that is, to call one of its methods), use the syntax **object.methodName(arguments)**. The value of this expression will be the value returned by the method (or null if no value is returned).

1.6 STATEMENTS

The most commonly used statements are assignment statements, blocks (or compound statements), if statements, while loops, and for loops. All statements except blocks must end with a semicolon. The println method may be used to produce output.

A **block** combines any number of statements into a single **compound statement** by enclosing them in braces, {}.

An **assignment statement** gives a value to a variable. If the variable has not previously been declared, the type must be specified; the variable can be used from the point of declaration to the end of the innermost enclosing block.

An **if statement** tests a boolean condition and executes a statement if the condition is true. It may have an else part, which will execute a different statement if the condition is false. Since each part controls a single statement, that statement is typically a block.

```
if (2 + 2 == 4) {
   System.out.println("All is well.");
} else {
   System.out.println("What??");
}
```

A while loop evaluates a boolean condition. If the condition is true, it executes a statement (usually a block), then comes back to the test. It exits when the test evaluates to false.

```
int count = 10;
while (count > 0) {
```

```
    System.out.println(count);
    count = count - 1;
}
System.out.println("Blast off!");
```

A for loop sets an initial value, tests a boolean condition, executes a statement if the condition is true, executes an update, and returns to the test. It exits when the test returns false.

```
for (int i = 10; i > 0; i = i - 1) {
    System.out.println(i);
}
System.out.println("Blast off!");
```

> **Note:** The above statements require a *boolean* condition to serve as a test. You cannot use a numeric value as a test.

The prevailing convention in the C family of languages is to put the opening brace of a block by itself at the beginning of a line. In Java, however, the style has always been to put the opening brace at the end of the line, as in the examples above. "When in Rome, do as the Romans do."

Java has no "print" statement, but the print and println *methods* can be used as if they were statements. System.out.println(*arg*) takes a single argument and sends it to standard output, followed by a *newline* character, '\n'. System.out.print(*arg*) does the same but without the newline.

1.7 PROGRAM EXECUTION

The value of a good **IDE** (**Integrated Development Environment**) cannot be overstated. NetBeans, Eclipse, IntelliJ IDEA, and Xcode (Mac only) are all excellent. Of these, IntelliJ IDEA may be the easiest for a beginner. Any IDE will provide a simple way to run your program.

The program will start execution at the main method of a public class. The main method should have this *exact* header:

```
public static void main(String[] args) {
```

If you are not using an IDE, any plain text editor (*not* a word processor) may be used to create a program. Each class should be on a separate file, and the name of the file should be the name of the class with the .java extension.

If you are using Java 11 or later, you can run a program by navigating to the folder containing the Java file and opening a command/terminal window. In that window, enter java *fileName*. The file should run and produce output.

If the above does not work, you may need to first compile the file and then run it. To do this, execute the pair of commands:

```
javac ClassName.java
java ClassName.class
```

If a program consists of multiple files, any file that is used by another file must be compiled before the file that uses it can be compiled.

1.8 HELLO WORLD

To begin programming as quickly as possible, you can use the following "Hello World" program as a framework. You don't need to understand it completely in order to get started.

```java
public class MyClass {
   String hello = "Hello World";
   public static void main(String[] args) {
      new MyClass().doSomething();
   }
   void doSomething() {
      System.out.println(hello);
   }
}
```

If saved on a file named MyClass.java, this program can be executed by following the instructions in the previous section.

There are two methods, main and doSomething. The program begins execution in the main method. The main method is in a "static context," which means it can't directly use any methods or variables that aren't also static. To get out of static context, main creates a new object of type MyClass and immediately calls its doSomething method; this is where you would put your code. After all this, you can forget about the word static until you have a use for it.

The declaration void doSomething() defines a **method** named doSomething. It takes no parameters, as indicated by the empty parentheses, and returns no value, as indicated by void. The method body is enclosed in braces, {}, and consists of a call to the method System.out.println with the argument hello. The println will print "Hello World" to **standard output**, which (depending on how you are running Java) should be somewhere on your screen.

Statements end with a semicolon. There are two statements in the above, one to call doSomething and one to print Hello World.

The names MyClass and doSomething (but not main) may be replaced with names of your choosing. By convention, class names always begin with a capital letter, and method names with a lowercase letter.

With HelloWorld as a starting point, you can add methods and code to make a useful program.

CHAPTER 2

Preliminaries

I T CAN BE USEFUL TO THINK OF JAVA as consisting of an "inner language" and an "outer language." The inner language consists of data, methods, and statements, and is all that is needed for a small program with only a single class. The equally complex outer language consists of all the various kinds of classes and interfaces used to organize a large program.

After some preliminaries, the next chapter describes the inner language of Java (which is very like C or C++), and the following chapter describes the outer language.

2.1 IDEs

> **Section summary:** The use of an IDE is strongly recommended. If you don't already use one, IntelliJ IDEA is one of the most beginner-friendly.

You can create and run complex Java programs with nothing more than a text editor and the command line, but this is doing things the hard way.

A professional *Integrated Development Environment* (*IDE*) is immeasurably helpful in developing programs. A very basic IDE integrates a text editor, a compiler, a debugger, and a code executor. A professional-level IDE will also suggest applicable methods, provide instant documentation lookup, offer corrections for mistakes, make automatic version backups, assist in reorganizing code, and any number of other services. I have had students tell me that they succeeded in my course only because their IDE wrote their programs for them.

The objection to a professional IDE is that it's a big, complicated program that's hard to learn (comparable to Microsoft Word, for example). This is undeniably true. My recommendation is to get a good, full-featured IDE and use it like a text editor that can run your programs. There is no need to learn all its features right away.

The most popular Java IDEs are *Eclipse, NetBeans, IntelliJ IDEA*, and the Mac-only *Xcode*. All are excellent and have ardent users; all have free versions. All can be (and are) used for a number of other languages. Of these, IntelliJ IDEA requires no prior knowledge of the interface but simply guides the beginning user at each step.

That said, sometimes an IDE will simply refuse to work. This could be the result of an upgrade, so that file versions are incompatible, or some similar problem. (I have had this problem a lot with Eclipse.) Reinstalling the IDE may help. Exploring all the possible settings may help. And, of course, you can switch to a different IDE.

There are simpler IDEs, often written specifically for students, such as *BlueJ, JCreator*, and *DrJava*. The advantage of a simpler IDE is that it is less intimidating. The disadvantage is that it does less to help the programmer.

It has been said that the hardest program to write in any language is "Hello World"; all subsequent programs are just elaborations of this one. In the same way, once you successfully use a professional IDE to write and execute a program, all the rest is just elaboration.

2.2 COMMENTS AND TAGS

There are three kinds of comments in Java.

- Comments beginning with // and continuing to the end of the line.
  - When placed at the end of a line of code, they say something about that line of code.

- When placed on a line by itself, they say something about the code that follows.

- Many IDEs will comment out an entire block of code by putting // at the beginning of each line.

- Comments beginning with /* and continuing up to */.

  - These are used for comments that won't fit on a single line, and they say something about the code that follows.

  - They may also be used to put a comment in the middle of a line of code.

- Comments beginning with /** and continuing up to */.

  - These are *documentation (doc) comments*. They are placed immediately before the declaration of a class, method, interface, or variable.

  - Doc comments are usually written with an asterisk at the beginning of each line after the first.

Documentation comments can contain *tags* such as @param and @return; many of these are described in Section 5.2.1.2, Javadoc.

Example:

```
/**
 * Returns the sum of two numbers.
 * @param a The first number.
 * @param b The second number. Cannot be negative.
 * @return the sum of the two numbers.
 * @throws AssertionError if b is negative.
 */
int add(int a, int b) {
    assert b >= 0; // ignored unless -ea is set
    while (b > 0) {
        // Move a 1 from b into a
        b -= 1;
        a += 1;
    }
```

```
    return a;
}
```

Javadoc is a program that extracts the information from doc comments and tags and produces very professional-looking documentation, usually but not necessarily as HTML. Non-doc comments are ignored.

CHAPTER 3

The "Inner Language" of Java

A JAVA PROGRAM CONSISTS OF ONE OR MORE CLASSES. This book uses "inner language," to mean what happens within a single, top-level class. For simple programs, one class may be all that is needed.

3.1 VARIABLES AND NAMING CONVENTIONS

A *variable* is a name that can be assigned a value. A variable can have different values at different times.

All variables must be declared. When a variable is declared, it is given a *type* that tells what kind of values it can have. It may also be given an initial value. An int variable can only have an integer value, a String variable can only have a character string as its value, and so on.

Java is case-sensitive; that is, result, Result, and RESULT are three different names. The names of the primitive types (int, double, etc.) are all lowercase, while object type names such as String are capitalized.

An *instance variable* is one that is declared in a class but a separate copy of it is "owned" by each individual *instance*, or object, of that class.

DOI: 10.1201/9781003402947-3

A *class variable*, or *static variable*, is declared in a class using the keyword static. There is only one of it, not one per object, and it is considered to be "owned" by the class itself, not by the individual objects.

A *local variable* is one that is declared within a method. It is available only within that method. *Parameters* to a method are also local to that method.

A *constant* is a "variable" whose value cannot be changed. It is indicated by adding the keyword final.

Many kinds of things in Java have names, not just variables. Proper naming and capitalization helps the experienced Java programmer know what kind of thing is being named. There are strong conventions for names:

- Variable names and method names are almost never abbreviated: Use employee rather than emp; use yearEndBonus rather than yebonus. (However, very common abbreviations can be used, such as max and min.)

- Variable names and method names always begin with a lowercase letter.

- Variable names and class names are usually nouns. Method names are usually verbs, or begin with a verb.

- If a name consists of multiple words, the first letter of all words except the first is capitalized, for example, firstName, totalCost. (One common name for this style is *camelCase*.)

- Although legal, variable names never contain the underscore (unless they are constants) or the dollar sign.

  - In Java 9 and later, underscores in names are discouraged (except for constants), and an underscore by itself is not a legal name.

- The names of constants are written in all capital letters. If the constant name consists of multiple words, underscores are used between the words. For example, END_OF_LINE_MARKER.

- Class names and interface names always begin with a capital letter, and multiword names are camel case.

3.2 BASIC DATA TYPES

There are eight *primitive* data types: char, byte, short, int, long, float, double, and boolean. All other values (arrays, strings, etc.) are of some class, or object, type. The distinction is important.

3.2.1 Primitive Types

Here are the four most important and most used primitive types:

- An int is an integer, or "whole number." It can hold numbers large enough for most purposes (about plus or minus two billion). To make very large numbers more readable, you can put underscores between digits.

- A double is a 64-bit "real" (floating point) number. It can hold very large and very small numbers, with about 17 digits of accuracy. It may be written in scientific notation, with e or E denoting the exponent: 6.0221409×10^{23} can be written as 6.0221409e+23. As with integers, you can put underscores between digits.

- A char is a single character. Common characters can be written simply by enclosing them in single quotes, for example, 'a'. Some characters need to be represented by escape sequences, such as '\n' for a newline.

- A boolean is a single true or false value.

The other four primitive types (long, short, byte, and float) aren't used in most programs, and will be discussed in section 5.2.2.6.

3.2.2 Arrays

An *array* is an ordered sequence of values, all of the same type. To access the individual values in an array, use the syntax *arrayName[index]*. Legal indices range from 0 (the first value in the array) to *arrayName*.length -1 (the last value).

The simplest syntax for *declaring* an array is either:

baseType[] arrayName;

or:

baseType arrayName[ ];

For example,

```
int[] scores;
```

This declares but does not define the scores variable. That is, its type has been assigned, but no value of that type has been assigned to it. An array variable that has been declared but defined will have the special value null, and attempting to use it will result in an error.

To both declare and define scores, you can say:

```
int[] scores = new int[35];
```

Once an array is defined, you cannot change its size. However, the size of an array is not part of its type, so an int array of any size can be assigned to scores. Later, you might assign a different array, of a different size, to scores. You can find the size of an array by asking it for its length variable, *array*.length.

Arrays created as shown above will have its elements set to 0, false, or null, for numeric, boolean, or object arrays, respectively. Alternatively, an array can be created with specific values, using the syntax new *type[ ]* {*value*, ...}, for example,

```
int[] ary = new int[] {3, 1, 4, 1, 6};
```

or with the slightly simpler

```
int[] ary2 = {3, 1, 4, 1, 6};
```

The values in an array can themselves be arrays. There is a special syntax for this, as in the following examples:

```
double elevation[][]; // declaration
```

```
elevation = new double[50][75]; // definition
elevation[49][74] = 123.45;
```

The elevation array can be referred to as a *two-dimensional array*, but it is more accurately thought of as a one-dimensional array whose elements happen to be arrays. Arrays may have three, four, or even more dimensions.

The first index in a multi-dimensional array is usually called the *row* number, and the second index the *column* number. The above array has 50 rows with indices 0 to 49, and 75 columns with indices 0 to 74.

The values in an array must all be of the same type, but the array size is not part of that type. The following code constructs a "triangular" array of arrays, in which each sub-array is larger than the one preceding it:

```
int[] triangle = new int[10];
for (int i = 0; i < triangle.length; i++) {
    triangle[i] = new int[i + 1];
}
```

3.2.3 Strings

A *string literal* is a sequence of zero or more characters enclosed in quotation (double quote) marks. For example:

```
""      // an empty string
"hello" // a string containing five characters
```

Some characters cannot be entered directly in a character or string constant; for example, double quotes within a string. These characters can be included by *escaping* them (putting a backslash in front of them):

```
"He said, \"Don't go.\""
```

The important *escape sequences* are:

- \n is a "newline" character, however that is encoded on your computer system (it is different on Windows than on Unix and Macintosh).

- \t is a tab character, representing an arbitrary amount of white space.

- \" is a double quote character (useful inside doubly-quoted strings).

- \" is a single quote character.

- \\ is a backslash character.

- \u*xxxx* is a Unicode character written as exactly four hex digits.

In addition, there are the seldom-used \b for backspace, \r for carriage return, and \f for form feed.

Although escape sequences have to be typed using two or more characters, each one counts as a single character, so "\"Who?\"".length() is 6.

> **Note:** Arrays have a length *field*, *array*.length, but Strings have a length *method*, *string*.length().

Strings literals are values, and can be saved in String variables:

```
String name = "We're doing Java";
```

Strings can be **concatenated**, or "pasted together," with the + operator:

```
String fullName = firstName + " " + lastName;
```

A value of any type, when concatenated ("added") to a string, is automatically converted to a string.

```
String message = "There are" + count + "errors.";
```

Strings are **immutable**, that is, you cannot change the length or the characters in a string; you can only create a new string.

3.2.4 Exceptions

Lots of things can go wrong in a program: dividing by zero, going outside the bounds of an array, reading a file that isn't there. When one of these things happens, Java creates a type of object called an Exception. There are many different subtypes of Exception, for example, ArithmeticException and the all-too-common NullPointerException.

Exceptions are objects, just like strings and arrays are objects, and there are two general kinds: **checked** and **unchecked.**

A checked exception is one that your program is required to deal with. For example, if you try to read a file, Java knows that there are a lot of things that could go wrong, and requires you to have code to handle it if they do. The usual way to handle it is with a try-catch-finally statement (see section 3.3.2.5). Basically, this statement says: "I'm going to *try* to do this, but if it doesn't work I will *catch* the exception and do something appropriate."

An unchecked exception is one that might happen, but you aren't required to check for it. These exceptions almost always result from bugs in your program, such as going outside the bounds of an array, or trying to use a null object. The solution is to debug the program.

3.2.5 Operators and Precedence

Java has the usual arithmetic operators, with the usual **precedence** (multiplications before additions, etc.). Operators with the highest precedence are done first and, with some exceptions, most operators are **left associative**—that is, operators with equal priority are done left to right. For example, 12 - 2 - 3 * 4 == 10 - 12 == -2.

The most common operators, from highest to lowest precedence, are:

- Method calls and array indexing
- Arithmetic operations:

    unary + and unary -

    * (multiplication), / (division), and % (remainder, or modulus)

    + (addition) and - (subtraction)

- Boolean (logical) operators:

    ! (not)

&& (and)

|| (or)

- Inequality tests:

    < <= >= > (less than, less or equal, greater or equal, greater than)

- Equality tests:

    == (equal to) and != (not equal to)

- Assignment operators:

    = (simple assignment)

    +=, -=, *=, /=, and %= (x *op*= y is short for x = x *op* y).

The unary and assignment operators are **right associative**—operators of equal precedence are done right-to-left. For example, a = b += c means a = (b += c).

As usual, parentheses can be used to explicitly specify an order of operations. There are a number of other operators in Java, but since very few programmers know the complete precedence table, it is better to use parentheses to make the order of operations clear.

Less important operators (++, --, ?:, and the shift and bit manipulation operators) will be discussed later—see sections 5.2.4.4 (++ and --), 5.2.4.2 (?:), and 5.2.4.3 (bit and shift), respectively.

When arithmetic is done using only integral types (including char), the result is an int. Arithmetic using a double with any numeric type results in a double.

The boolean operations && and || are **short-circuit operations**: If the result is known after evaluating the left operand, the right operand is not evaluated. Thus, in the expression f(x) && g(x), if f(x) is false then the result has to be false, so g(x) is not evaluated. Similarly, in the expression f(x) || g(x), if f(x) is true then the result has to be true, so g(x) is not evaluated.

3.2.6 Declarations and Casting

Every variable must be declared, along with its type and an optional initial value. For example,

- `int count = 0, size;`

- `double min, max, average;`

- `char c;`

Java will complain if it thinks you might be using a variable before it has been given a value. If Java doesn't catch this mistake, the value used will be zero for numeric types or `false` for booleans.

A char variable can hold any of about 65000 UTF-16 characters (see section 5.2.2.4). Characters are stored internally as numbers, and can be used in arithmetic as if they were integers. You can write a UTF-16 character in hexadecimal as `'\uxxxx'`, where **xxxx** is a hexadecimal number in the range `'\u0000'` to `'\uffff'`. For example, `'\u0041'` is `'A'`, and `'\u03A3'` is `'Σ'`.

Among the above types, a double is considered to be **wider** than an int, and an int is wider than a char. A value of one type can be assigned to a variable of a wider type. That is, a char value can be assigned to an int variable or a double variable, and an int variable can be assigned to a double variable. This is called **upcasting**.

To go in the other direction, that is, to assign a wider value to a narrower type of variable, you must **cast** (or **downcast**) the value to the desired type. Do this by putting the name of the desired type in parentheses immediately before the value. For example,

```
int i = 0;
double d = 2.71828;
i = (int)d;
System.out.println(i); // prints 2
```

In the above example, the fractional part is lost.

A cast affects the *one* immediately following value: (int)2 * d casts only the 2 to an int (which it already is). To cast an expression, put parentheses around it: (int)(2 * d).

As another example, consider:

```
char ch = (char)('a' + 1); // result is 'b'
```

The cast is necessary because the result type of 'a' + 1 is int.

When casting to a narrower type, it is the programmer's responsibility to ensure that the value will fit in that narrower type, or the results will be quite unexpected. For example, a byte can hold only values between −128 and 127, but the cast (byte)1000 is legal and results in −24.

A boolean is *not* a numeric type, and cannot be cast to or from any other type.

3.2.7 Constants

Putting the word final in front of a variable declaration makes it into a *constant*; its value cannot be changed. For example,

```
final int DAYS_IN_A_WEEK = 7;
```

Java provides some built-in constants, such as Math.PI and Math.E.

Constants help avoid the use of "magic numbers"—numbers in code whose meaning may not be absolutely clear. If the code adds 29 to a variable, the question arises, why 29?

However, it is silly to name a constant after its value, for example,

```
final int TWELVE = 12;
```

because this does nothing to improve the clarity of the code.

3.2.8 Methods

A method is like a function, except that it belongs to a class. This gives it special access to the variables and other methods of that class. The syntax is

```
/**
 * documentation comment
 */
access returnType methodName(parameterList) {
    declarations
    statements
}
```

There is no special keyword to begin the definition of a method. A method definition consists of:

1. An optional **documentation comment** to tell the user what the method does and how to use it.

2. An optional **access** specifier (see section 4.1.2). Default is *package* access.

3. The **return type** of value to be returned by the method, or void if the method does not return a value.

4. The **method name**. Method names should begin with a lowercase letter.

5. A parenthesized, comma-separated **parameter list**. If there are no parameters, the parentheses must still be present. Each parameter consists of:

   • The type of value expected for that parameter, and

   • The name of the parameter.

6. The body of the method, consisting of a pair of braces, {}, containing any number of declarations and executable statements.

Here is an example:

```
/**
 * A leap year is a year divisible by 4 but not
```

```
 * by 100, unless it is also divisible by 400.
 */
boolean isLeapYear(int year) {
   if (year % 4!= 0) return false;
   if (year % 100!= 0) return true;
   return year % 400 == 0;
}
```

In the body of the method you can have ***declarations*** of variables, with or without an initial value, for example,

```
int count = 0;
```

All such declarations are ***local*** to the method, that is, they can be seen and used only within the method. Variable declarations are usually put first in the method body. A method may make use of the values given to its parameters, its local variables, and any ***fields*** defined by the class it is in.

> **Note:** If a parameter or local variable has the same name as a field of the class, it will ***shadow*** (hide) the field. This is commonly done in constructors, and can be done for similar purposes in methods.

To make a complete program, there must be at least one "starting" class that contains the following special method:

```
public static void main(String[] args) { … }
```

There can be multiple methods with the same name, so long as they have different numbers of parameters or different parameter types. Java looks at both the name and the parameters (but not the return type) to decide which method to use.

If the method is declared to return a value of a certain type, it must use a `return` statement with a value of the correct type (or a value that can be widened to the correct type). It may not reach the end of the method without executing a `return` statement.

Within the method, the **statements** can refer to any fields of the class, any parameters, and any local declarations. The keyword this refers to "this" object, the one executing the method. When there is a local variable or parameter with the same **name** as a field, then **name** by itself refers to the local variable or parameter, while this. **name** refers to the field.

> **Note to Python programmers:** The keyword this is like self in Python. The two differences are that this is a keyword, not a variable name, and that the word this can usually be omitted.

If a method is declared to be void (have no return value), then the method can finish either by executing return; with no value specified, or by reaching the end of the method.

> **Note:** void is not a value, so return void; is not allowed

3.2.9 Methods Calling Methods

Methods belong to objects, so to "call" a method, you technically "send a message to an object." Do this by naming the object, putting a dot, then putting the name of the method and, in parentheses, the correct number and types of **arguments**. Each argument is an expression (possibly a single value or variable).

obj . *methodName*(*arguments*)

There must be one argument for each parameter, and it must be of a type that can be assigned to that parameter. The called method returns a result that can be used in further expressions.

When a method calls another method in the same class (so that the object is "talking to itself"), the **obj** can be the keyword this, or it can be omitted. For example, if isLeapYear is in the same class as printLengthOfYear, then in printLengthOfYear you can say either this.isLeapYear(year) or simply isLeapYear(year).

```java
public void printLengthOfYear(int year) {
    int days = 365;
    if (isLeapYear(year)) { // "this." omitted
```

```
        days = 366;
    }
    System.out.println(year + " has " +
                        days + " days.");
}
```

3.2.10 Overloading

Methods may be **overloaded**. That is, a class can have two or more methods with the same name, so long as the methods have a different *number* of parameters or different *types* of parameters. For example, a class might have two or more methods named bump.

The types do not have to match up exactly. If there is no exact match, but the argument(s) can be widened to an appropriate type, then the method can be used. For example, the bump(int *n*) method could be called with char argument, but not with a double argument.

If we were to add a bump(char *n*) method, then a bump message with a char argument would call this new method, not the one expecting an int argument.

Constructors, like methods, can be overloaded.

Many of the methods provided by Java are overloaded. For example, there are nine versions of System.out.print(*arg*) and ten of System.out.println(*arg*). These methods have a separate version for each of boolean, char, double, float, int, long, Object, String, and char[]. (No separate versions are provide for byte and short, because these can be widened and used by the int method.) There is one additional version of println that takes no argument, and prints a blank line.

3.2.11 Scope

Every variable has a *scope*, which is the part of the program in which the variable may be used. The scope depends on where the variable is declared.

3.2.11.1 Variables Declared in Classes

Variables that are declared within a class are available everywhere within the class. If a variable is declared with an initial value, that value may be used in subsequent declarations.

```
public class MyClass {
    int x = 5;
    int y = x + 1; // can use x here
    int z = w + 1; // but this is illegal
    // now we can use x, y, and z
    int w = 3;
    // now we can also use w
    ...
}
```

Here's one way to think of it. When a class is first used, Java goes through and executes all the top-level declarations (that is, those not in methods), in the order that they appear. After that, the methods in the class are available for use.

Exception: static methods in a class (such as the main method) can only use static variables in that class.

3.2.11.2 Variables Declared in Methods

A **block** or **compound statement** is a group of declarations and/or statements enclosed in braces, {}.

A **method** consists of a **header** and a **body**; the body is a **block**.

```
public double average(double x, double y) {
    double sum = x + y;
    return sum / 2;
}
```

The parameters (in this example, x and y) can be used everywhere in the method, but are not available outside the method. Variables declared within the body (sum in this example) follow the scope rules for blocks (see the next section).

The parameters and the variables declared within the body are **local variables**; they are created when the method is invoked (used), and discarded when the method returns. Local variables do not retain their values from one invocation (call) of the method to the next; each invocation starts all over again.

3.2.11.3 Variables Declared in Blocks

A variable declared within a block is accessible (can be used) from the point of declaration to the end of the block. For example:

```
{
    x = 1; // illegal!
    int x; // scope of "x" starts here
    x = 2; // legal
} // scope of "x" ends here
x = 3; // illegal!
```

Variable declarations are usually put first in a block.

3.3 STATEMENT TYPES

Java and C++ both borrowed heavily from the C language, and many of the statement types are identical.

One significant difference is that, in Java, the **condition** (test) of an `if`, `for`, `while`, or `do-while` statement *must* be an expression that results in a boolean value, not any other type.

Java is usually formatted to put the opening brace of a control statement on the same line as the control statement, and the closing brace aligned with the control statement (see below for examples). In addition, Java programmers are encouraged to use braces even when the block consists of only a single statement.

> **Note:** Statements may be labeled for access by break and continue statements (see sections 3.3.1.1 and 3.3.1.12), but there is no goto statement.

The following statements are not in C++, or differ significantly from those in C++. See section 3.3.2 for detailed descriptions.

- `assert` *booleanExpression*;
- `assert` *booleanExpression*: *expression*;
- `switch` (*expression*) {

```
      case labels₁ -> action₁
      case labels₂ -> action₂
      ...
      case labelsₙ -> actionₙ
      default -> actiondef
   }
```

- System.out.println(*value*);

- System.out.print(*value*);

- try {
      statements
   }
   catch (*ExceptionType variable*) {
      statements
   } // there may be multiple catch clauses
   finally {
      statements
   }

- throw *Exception*;

Here is a list of the statements that are essentially the same as those in C++.

- *variable* = *expression*;

- *expression;*

- { *statements* }

- if (*condition*) {
      statements
   }

- if (*condition*) {
      statements₁
   } else {
      statements₂
   }

- while (*condition*) {
      statements
   }

- for (*initialization*; *condition*; *update*) {
      statements
  }

- for (*variable: collection*) {
      statements
  }

- do {
      statements
  } while (*condition*)

- switch (*expression*) {
    case *value$_1$*:
        statements$_1$
    case *value$_2$*:
        statements$_2$
    ...
    default:
        statements$_{def}$
  }

- *label*: *statement*;

- break;

- break *label*;

- continue;

- continue *label*;

- return *value*;

- return;

- ; // empty statement

3.3.1 Statements Also in C++

If you are coming from C++ or one of the other C type languages, you probably already know everything in this section. It's all the normal loops, conditional statements, assignments, blocks, and so forth. Feel free to skip ahead to section 3.3.2, Statements Not In C++.

3.3.1.1 Blocks

A **compound statement**, or **block**, is some number (possibly zero) of declarations and statements, enclosed in braces, {}.

Control statements, such as `if` statements and loops, control the execution of a single statement. If you want to control more than just one statement, you must enclose those statements in braces, `{}`, to make them into a (single) compound statement.

> **Style:** Standard Java style is to put an opening brace at the end of a line, never on a line by itself. The closing brace should be indented the same amount as the line containing the opening brace.

The body of a class or method must always be a block.

Good style dictates that statements within a block be indented relative to the start of the block. The usual indentation for Java is four spaces.

3.3.1.2 Assignment Statements

An **assignment statement** assigns a value to a variable. For example, if x is of type `int`, then

```
x = 5;
```

gives x the value 5.

The value of a variable, but not its type, may be changed. For example, the assignment statement

```
x = 10;
```

will give x the new value 10.

For each arithmetic operator **op**, the expression

> **variable op= expression;**

is shorthand for

> **variable = variable op expression;**

For example, x += 1; adds 1 to x.

3.3.1.3 Method Calls and Varargs

Method calls can be used as statements, because they can have side effects. For example, if a is an array, a.sort() sorts the array.

Methods that have no side effects should not be used as statements, because they don't do anything. If str is the string "Hello", the expression str.toUpperCase() *returns* the string "HELLO", and this can be assigned to a variable, but does not change the value of str. Hence, using str.toUpperCase() as a statement does nothing.

You can write a method that takes a variable number of arguments, or *varargs*. Simply put three dots after the type name of the *last* parameter. When the method is called, Java puts all those last values into an array for you.

```java
public double average(double… args) {
    double sum = 0;
    for (double arg: args) {
        sum += arg;
    }
    return sum / args.length;
}
```

The call average(10.0, 20.0, 30, 41.0) will return 25.25.

3.3.1.4 If Statements

An if statement tests a condition. If the condition is true, the following statement (typically, a compound statement) is executed. If the condition is not true, the if statement does nothing. The syntax is:

```java
if (condition) {
    statements
}
```

For example, the following if statement resets x to zero if it has become negative.

```java
if (x < 0) {
    x = 0;
}
```

An if statement may also have an else clause. If the condition is true, the statement following the condition is executed. If the condition is not true, the statement following the keyword else is executed. Both statements are typically compound statements. The syntax is:

```
if (condition) {
    some statements
}
else {
    some other statements
}
```

For example,

```
if (x % 2 == 0) {
    x = x / 2;
}
else {
    x = 3 * x + 1
}
```

It is good style to always use the braces, even if they include only a single statement. However, if either part contains just one (non-compound) statement, it is legal to omit the braces. If you do this, you should put the single statement on the same line as the if or the else.

```
if (x % 2 == 0) x = x / 2;
else x = 3 * x + 1;
```

Java, unlike Python, has no single keyword as an abbreviation for else if.

```
if (x < 0) {
    System.out.println("x is negative");
} else if (x > 0) {
    System.out.println("x is positive");
} else {
    System.out.println("x is zero");
}
```

3.3.1.5 While Loops

A while loop is a loop with the test at the top. The syntax is:

```
while (condition) {
    statements
}
```

First, the *condition* is tested; if it is false, nothing more is done, and the loop exits without ever executing the *statements*. If the *condition* is true, the *statements* are executed, then the entire loop (starting with the test) is executed again.

For example, the number of digits in a nonzero number can be computed by:

```
int countDigits(int number) {
    int count = 0;
    while (number != 0) {
        number = number / 10;
        count += 1;
    }
    return count;
}
```

The braces indicate a block of statements. If there is only one statement, the braces may be omitted; however, it is good style to always include the braces.

Normally, the statements controlled by the loop must affect the condition being tested. In the above example, number is compared to 0, and the statements in the loop change the value of number. If the controlled statements never make the condition false, then the loop never exits, and the program "hangs" (stops responding). This is a kind of error is commonly, if inaccurately, called an *infinite loop*.

Two additional statement types, break and continue (see sections 3.3.1.11 and 3.3.1.12), can also control the behavior of while loops. These statements can be used with statement labels.

3.3.1.6 Do-while Loops

A do-while loop is a loop with the test at the bottom, rather than the more usual test at the top. The syntax is:

```
do {
    statements
} while (condition);
```

First, the **statements** are executed, then the **condition** is tested; if it is true, then the entire loop is executed again. The loop exits when the **condition** gives a false result.

This kind of loop is most often used when the test doesn't make any sense until the loop body has been executed at least once. For most purposes, the while loop is preferable.

For example, suppose you want to choose a random number between 0 and 1000 that is divisible by 7. You cannot test the number until after you have chosen it, so do-while is appropriate.

```
Random rand = new Random();
int x;
do {
    x = rand.nextInt(1000);
} while (x % 7 != 0);
```

As with a while loop, an infinite loop will result if the exit condition is never satisfied.

The do-while loop is a little harder to think about than a while loop. Since we want a number that *is* divisible by 7, the loop has to test that the number *is not* divisible by 7.

Unlike other kinds of control statement, the braces in a do-while are required, even if only a single statement is in the loop.

The following code does *not* work:

```
do {
    int x = rand.nextInt(1000);
} while (x % 7 != 0); // error
```

Variables declared within a block are local to that block. If the variable x is declared within the braces of the do-while loop, it cannot be used in the condition, which lies outside of the block.

Two additional statement types, break and continue, can also control the behavior of do-while loops. These statements can be used with statement labels.

3.3.1.7 Traditional For Loops

A for loop is a loop with the test at the top. The syntax is:

```
for (initialization; condition; update) {
    statements
}
```

The *initialization* is performed first, and only once. After that, the *condition* is tested and, if true, the *statements* are executed and the *update* is performed; then control returns to the *condition*. In other words, the for loop behaves almost exactly like the following while loop:

```
initialization;
while (condition) {
    statements;
    update;
}
```

The *initialization* is typically either an assignment to a previously declared variable, for example, i = 0, or a combined declaration and assignment, for example, int i = 0. The *update* is typically an assignment statement such as i += 1.

The scope of any variable declared in the *initialization* (that is, where the variable can be used), is the entire for statement.

The braces indicate a block of **statements**. If there is only one statement, the braces may be omitted; however, it is good style to always include the braces.

As an example, an array can be declared and its contents written out by:

```
int[] ary = {3, 1, 4, 1, 6};
for (int i = 0; i < ary.length; i += 1) {
   System.out.println(ary[i]);
}
```

Also legal, but much less commonly used, the **initialization** and the **update** may each consist of two or more assignments. For example,

```
for (int i = 1, j = 100; i < j; i = 2 * i, j -= 1) {
   System.out.println("i = " + i + ", j = " + j);
}
```

Two additional statement types, `break` and `continue`, can also control the behavior of `for` loops. These statements, described in sections 3.3.1.11 and 3.3.1.12, can be used with statement labels.

3.3.1.8 For-each Loop

A for-each loop does not involve any explicit testing; it simply goes through every element of an array, in order. This is simpler and more convenient when the index location of the elements is not needed. The syntax is:

for (*type variable*: *array*) { *statements* }

As with a traditional `for` loop, the *type* must be omitted if the variable has been previously declared. Also, as with the traditional `for` loop, the scope of the *variable* is the entire `for` statement. For example, every element in a String array names can be printed out as follows:

```
for (String name: names) {
   System.out.println(name);
}
```

The for-each loop can also be used with iterable objects (see section 5.2.3.1).

3.3.1.9 Classic switch Statements

Just as the if statement provides a choice between two blocks of code, based on a boolean value, the switch statement provides a choice between several blocks of code, based on an integer, character, string, or Enum value.

> **Note:** This section describes the "traditional" switch statement, available in all versions of Java. For the newer (and better) version available in Java 14 and beyond, see section 3.3.2.3.

The syntax is fairly complex:

```
switch (expression) {
    case constant₁:
        statements₁;
        break;
    case constant₂:
        statements₂;
        break;
    ...
    case constant_N:
        statements_N;
        break;
    default:
        statements_def;
}
```

Operation is as follows. The **expression** is evaluated, then compared to each case **constant** in order. When a **constant** is found that is equal to the **expression**, execution begins with the following statements, and continues until either a break or a return is encountered, or until the end of the entire switch statement.

The value of the expression must be one of the integer types (including char), or a string, or an Enum value (see section 5.3.6). The **constants** may be integers, characters, literal strings, or Enum values.

The break statement is not required at the end of each case, just strongly recommended. Without a break, control will "fall through" into the next group of statements. This is seldom what you want to happen. On the rare occasion that this really is the desired behavior, you should include a comment that the omission is intentional, otherwise you or someone else may "correct" this apparent problem at some later date.

If the same code should be executed for one or more constants, rather than duplicating the code, one case *constant*: can be followed immediately by the next, for example,

```
case "yes":
case "Yes":
case "YES":
    some statements
```

In Java 14 and later, the above can be abbreviated to

```
case "yes", "Yes", "YES": some statements.
```

The default case is optional, and should come last; it will be executed if no earlier matching *expression* is found. If no matching *expression* is found and there is no default case, the switch statement exits without doing anything.

It is good style always to include a default case, even if you believe that all possibilities have been covered. The default case might be empty, or it could include the statement assert false; to indicate that this code should never be reached. (Assert statements are covered in section 3.3.2.1.)

The *statements* may be any sequence of zero or more statements. It is not necessary to use braces to group the statements (including the following break statement) into a compound statement, although this is sometimes done.

Here is a contrived example:

```
int i = 3;
String s;
switch (i) {
   case 1:
      s = "one";
      break;
   case 2:
      s = "two";
      break;
   default:
      s = "many";
}
```

This will result in s being set to "many".

3.3.1.10 Labeled Statements

The syntax of a labeled statement is

identifier: **statement**;

Any statement may be labeled with an identifier, but it really only makes sense to label loop statements and switch statements. Labels are used in conjunction with the break and continue statements.

3.3.1.11 Break Statements

A break statement is used to prematurely exit the immediately enclosing loop (of any kind) or switch statement.

It can also be used to exit nested loops and/or switch statements. To do this, put a *label* (see previous section) on the loop or switch statement you want to exit, and put the label after the word break:

break **label**;

Given an array of numbers, consider the problem of finding two different numbers such that one is exactly ten times the other. The following code solves this problem.

```
int i, j = 0;
int[] ary = {7, 30, 9, 20, 3, 5};
id: for (i = 0; i < ary.length; i += 1) {
   for (j = 0; j < ary.length; j += 1) {
      if (i != j && ary[i] == 10 * ary[j]) {
         break id;
      }
   }
}
System.out.println(ary[i] + ", " + ary[j]);
```

Some programmers dislike the break statement, and indeed, there is usually a better way to solve a problem without using it.

3.3.1.12 Continue Statements

A continue statement is used to go from the middle of a loop to the beginning of the next time through the loop. That is, the continue statement causes the enclosing loop to return to the test of a while loop, to the increment and test of a for loop, or to the beginning of a do-while loop.

If the continue statement is within nested loops, it can be used to go to the beginning of a particular loop. To do this, put a label on the desired loop, and put that label after the word continue.

```
continue label;
```

The following code computes the average of the positive values in the array ary, ignoring the zero and negative values.

```
int[] ary = {10, 20, 5, -1, 30, -12, 50};
double sum = 0;
int count = 0;

for (int i = 0; i < ary.length; i += 1) {
   if (ary[i] <= 0) continue;
   sum += ary[i];
   count += 1;
}
double average = sum / count;
```

While there is nothing actually wrong with the continue statement, refactoring the code to remove it almost always results in a simpler and more understandable program.

3.3.1.13 Return Statements

When a method is defined, it must specify the type of the value to be returned. If no value is to be returned, the keyword void must be used in place of a type name, and the use of a return statement is optional. Examples:

```java
int add(int a, int b) {
   return a + b;
}
void print(int x) {
   System.out.println(x);
   return; // superfluous
}
```

The syntax of the return statement is either simply

```java
return;
```

for a void method, or

```java
return expression;
```

for a method that returns a value. The type of the *expression* must be the same as, or narrower than, the type that the method is supposed to return.

For example, if a method is supposed to return a double value, the return statement may use an int expression; the result will be converted to a double as the method returns.

3.3.1.14 Empty Statements

Although of very limited use, Java does allow the use of an "empty" statement, consisting of a semicolon by itself. The following statements are equivalent:

```java
for (n = 1; n < 1000; n = 2 * n) {}
```

and

```
for (n = 1; n < 1000; n = 2 * n);
```

Either statement results in n being set to 1024.

3.3.2 Statements Not in C++

The following statements are either not in C++ at all, or they are sufficiently different to warrant additional explanation.

3.3.2.1 Assert Statements

The assert statement is unusual in that it usually "doesn't do anything." Rather, it is a form of executable documentation: you are *asserting* that something is true. There are two forms:

```
assert booleanExpression;
assert booleanExpression : expression;
```

Execution is as follows. The **booleanExpression** is evaluated, and if true, control just passes to the next statement. But if it is false, an AssertionError is thrown. If the second form is used, the value of the **expression** (which may be any type) is included in the error message.

By default, assertions are treated like comments. To make assert statements executable, use the VM flag -enableassertions or its abbreviation -ea.

> **Note:** When running from a command line, **VM** (**Virtual Machine**) flags may be placed after the word java. When running from an IDE, flags will be a configuration option.

The purpose of the assert statement is to state some condition that you believe will always be true at that point in the program. It should not be used to check for possible error conditions that you believe could happen; for that, you should throw an exception (see section 3.3.2.6).

It is a good idea to get into the habit of putting in assert statements, as appropriate, when you write the code.

There is little point in using the second form (with **expression**) unless you have something useful to add. For example, if you believe that some array index i is always within the array bounds, you might say

```
assert i >= 0 && i < myArray.length:
  "Bad array index:" + i;
```

Finally, the idiom `assert false;` can be used to indicate that you believe that a certain section of code (for example, the default case of a switch statement) can never be reached. However, it is a syntax error to put this (or any other) statement in a location that the Java compiler knows cannot be reached, such as immediately following a return statement.

3.3.2.2 Print "Statements"
There are two "statements" that can print a message to the user. They are

```
System.out.println(value);
```

and

```
System.out.print(value);
```

The difference is that `print` just prints a string representation of the **value**, while `println` prints that string followed by a newline character. That is, the next thing printed after a `print` will be on the same line, but the next thing printed after a `println` will be on a new line.

Although `print` and `println` are used as if they were statements, they are actually methods that have the **side effect** of displaying something on your screen. (Method calls which do not have side effects can also be used as statements, but this is usually pointless, since the return value is ignored.)

If the **value** is an object type, `print` and `println` will call its `toString` method to get a printable representation of the object. This gives you considerable control over how your objects are printed (see section 4.4.1).

It is often convenient to construct a string (using "+" to join the parts) directly in the parameter list of a call to print or println. Anything "added" to a string will be converted to a string.

```
System.out.println("The sum is" + sum);
```

> **Technical note:** System is the name of a class in the java.lang package, and out is an object of type PrintStream in the System class. The PrintStream class has several methods, including print and println. You don't need to know this in order to use the methods.

Printing to the screen is easy, but getting input from the keyboard requires the use of a Scanner object, covered in section 3.4.1.3.

3.3.2.3 Switch Statements and Expressions

Java 14 introduced a significantly improved version of the switch statement. (The old version is still available.) The new version can be used either as a statement or as an *expression* that returns a value. The syntax is:

```
switch (expression) {
    case constants₁ -> action₁
    case constants₂ -> action₂
    ...
    case constantsN -> actionN
    default -> actiondef
}
```

The *expression* must result in an integer, String, or Enum value.

The *constants* are comma-separated lists of one or more values of the same type as *expression*. Constants may not be duplicated.

The switch, whether used as a statement or as an expression, evaluates the *expression*, chooses a case whose *constant* is equal to that of *expression*, and executes the one *action* associated with that constant. If no constant matches, the default action is executed.

> **Note:** Unlike the "classic" switch statement, there is no "fall through" to the next action.

When switch is used as a statement, each **action** is a single statement, possibly a compound statement. The default case is optional; if no constant is matched and there is no default case, the statement does nothing.

When switch is used as an expression, each **action** may be

- An expression of the correct type to be used as the value of the switch.

- A compound statement, containing a statement of the form yield **expression**. The yield acts rather like a return statement in a method; it causes the switch to exit with the expression as its value.

- A throw statement.

When switch is used as an expression, it *must* either return a value or throw an exception. In practical terms, this means that either the default case is required, or the **constants** include every possible value of an Enum.

The following nonsensical example illustrates the use of switch as an expression.

```
long nonsense = switch (i) {
    case 1 -> 1000000000000L;
    case 2 -> 17 * x;
    case 3, 4 -> 'a';
    case 5 -> {
        System.out.println("Five!");
        yield 55;
    }
    case 6 -> throw new RuntimeException();
    default -> -1;
};
System.out.println(nonsense);
```

3.3.2.4 Pattern Matching in switch Statements

As mentioned in the previous section, Java 14 introduced a new form of the switch statement, as well as a switch *expression*, using arrows (->)

instead of colons (:). Java 17 greatly expands what `switch` statements and expressions can do, using pattern matching.

> **Warning:** Pattern matching is a *preview feature* of Java 17. This means (1) it may change or disappear in future versions of Java, and (2) you may have to set the `enable-preview` flag in order to use it.

Despite the name, pattern matching has nothing to do with regular expressions. Instead, the switching is done on the *type* of an expression, and the result of the expression is assigned to a new variable.

```
switch (expression) {
    case Type1 variable1 -> action1
    case Type2 variable2 -> action2
    ...
    case TypeN variableN -> actionN
    default -> actiondef
}
```

The value of the *expression* must be a supertype of the case *Types*. When a matching *Type* is found, the value of the *expression* is assigned to the corresponding *variable*, and the *action* (expression or statement) is executed.

Unlike earlier versions of the `switch` statement, *any* object type may be used as a case type, including `null`. Primitives, however, cannot be used.

A *guarded pattern* allows us to perform an additional test on the value, after its type has been selected. This has the form

```
    case Type variable && guard -> action
```

where the *guard* is a boolean expression using the value of the *variable*. If the boolean expression is complicated, it should be enclosed in parentheses.

Here's an example, using a `switch` expression.

```
String s = switch (shape) {
  case Rectangle r && r.width == r.height ->
    "It's a square';
  case Rectangle r ->
    'It's a rectangle';
  case Triangle t ->
    'It's a' + t.width + 'by' +
    t.height + 'triangle.';
  default -> 'It's a shape.';
};
System.out.println(s);
```

3.3.2.5 Try-catch-finally

Code that can throw a checked exception must either be in a method that is declared to throw that exception, or it must be in the `try` part of a `try-catch-finally` statement. Syntax is as follows:

```
try {
    code that might throw the exception
}
catch (SomeExceptionType variable) {
    code to handle this kind of exception
}
catch (SomeOtherExceptionType variable) {
    code to handle this other exception type
}
finally {
    code that is always done before leaving
}
```

There may be as many `catch` blocks as desired, to catch different types of exceptions; the `finally` block is usually optional. But if there are no `catch` blocks, a `finally` block is required.

First, the code in the `try` block is executed. If it completes normally (without an exception or error), the `catch` blocks are skipped. But if an exception or error occurs while executing the `try` block, execution goes immediately to the first `catch` block that can handle that kind of exception.

Whether or not the code in the try block completes normally, the finally block (if present) is *always* executed. If the code in the try block or one of the catch blocks attempts to exit some other way (via a return, break, or continue statement), the finally block "steps in the way" and executes before that exit statement can occur.

3.3.2.6 Throw Statements

When Java detects that an error has occurred, it creates an Exception object and *throws* it. Your code can also deliberately create and throw exceptions. Typically you would create a new exception in the throw statement.

```
throw new ExceptionType(message);
```

> **Note:** This differs from C++ in that, in Java, only Throwable types (Exceptions and Errors) can be thrown.

In this section we consider only one simple example.

Suppose that if variable b is negative, it means something has gone wrong. You might write:

```
if (b < 0) {
    throw new Exception("b is negative");
}
```

This code creates an object of the very general type Exception (there are many more specific exception types) and immediately throws the Exception.

Some exception types are **checked.** If you execute code that could possibly throw a checked exception, Java insists that you do something about it; it is a syntax error if you don't. One thing you can do is to put the offending code in the try part of a try-catch statement.

Alternatively, you can say that your method (possibly) throws the exception. Then whatever called your code has to deal with the exception; it's no longer your responsibility.

```
int myMethod(int a, int b) throws Exception {
   if (b < 0) {
      throw new Exception("b is negative");
   }
   // other stuff
}
```

Now the code that calls myMethod must either call it in the try part of a try-catch statement, or the header of that calling method must include a throws part. In this way the exception may be passed up many levels of method calls before it is finally handled. If it reaches all the way up to the main method and the main method doesn't handle it, the program terminates with an error.

> **Note:** One special group of exceptions, the RuntimeException and its subclasses, are *unchecked* exceptions; that is, they do not have to be caught or mentioned in the method header. Unchecked exceptions are usually the result of an error in the program.

Exceptions in Java are complicated and expensive, so they should be reserved for handling problem situations; they should not be used as part of the "normal" flow of control.

3.3.3 Reading from a File

The basic approach to reading from or writing to a text file is (1) open the file, (2) use the file, and (3) close the file. Each of these steps could raise an exception which must be handled.

The FileReader class has methods that will read characters and return them as integers. This is inconvenient, so the usual way to read files is to wrap a BufferedReader around a FileReader object.

A BufferedReader has the following methods (among others):

- readLine() reads and returns one line (as a String), or null if the end of the file has been reached.

- read(*charArray*, *index*, *n*) fills the character array with *n* characters, starting at *index*. The return value is the number of characters actually read.

- close() closes both the BufferedReader and the associated FileReader. Closing an already-closed reader does not throw an exception.

Aside from dealing with exceptions, a BufferedReader can be used like this:

```
FileReader fr = new FileReader(file);
BufferedReader br = new BufferedReader(fr);
String line = br.readLine();
br.close();
```

The *file* argument to the FileReader constructor may be either a File object or a string representing a path to the file. If the file doesn't exist, the constructor will throw an FileNotFoundException.

The constructor for a BufferedReader will not throw an IOException, but any use of readLine, read, or close could do so.

3.3.4 Try With Resources

The *try-with-resources statement* is an extension of the try-catch-finally statement that provides a more convenient way of closing resources after using them. Instead of writing

```
try { ... }
```

write

```
try (resource declarations) { ... }
```

There may be any number of (closable) resource declarations, separated by semicolons. For example,

```
try (FileReader fr = new FileReader("/Users/dave/test.txt");
    BufferedReader br = new BufferedReader(fr);) {
```

```
    String line = br.readLine();
    System.out.println(line);
}
catch (IOException e) { }
```

With this construction, the FileReader and BufferedReader will be automatically closed after use, whether or not an exception has occurred.

If this code occurs in a method that is marked as throwing an IOException, the catch clause is not required. A finally clause is optional but not usually needed.

> **Note:** The above path has the form it does because this code was tested on a Macintosh. On a Windows machine, paths typically begin with C: and use double backslashes rather than forward slashes.

Java 9 introduced a shorter version of the try-with-resources statement that is sometimes useful. In this version, if the resources have been previously declared and are final or "effectively final," they can simply be named. For example, if BufferedReader br and FileReader fr have already been defined and are effectively final, then the following simpler form works:

```
try (br; fr) {
    line = br.readLine();
    System.out.println(line);
}
catch (IOException e) { }
```

> **Note:** A variable is *final* if it has been declared with the final keyword. A variable is *effectively final* if there is no code to change it after it has been declared.

3.3.5 Writing to a File

To write to a text file, you can use a FileWriter, which has a write (*string*) method and a close() method. The following example uses a try-with-resources statement to automatically close the file.

```
try (FileWriter fw = new FileWriter(
    "/Users/dave/test2.txt")) {
  fw.write("Hello\n");
  fw.write("Goodbye");
} catch (IOException e) {}
```

The above code segment will create the file test2.txt if it does not already exist, and will replace any existing contents of that file with the two lines Hello and Goodbye. To add to the end of an existing text file, use FileWriter's append(*string*) method.

3.4 CLASSES AND OBJECTS

A Java program consists of some number of **objects** interacting with one another, yet all executable code is in **classes**. So, what is the relationship between classes and objects?

Simply, each class defines a type, and objects are values of that type. Here is an analogy: A *class* is like a recipe, while *objects* are the things you can make by following the recipe. Once you have the recipe (class), you can make many things (objects) from it. Almost everything in a class is devoted to describing what is in the object, and what it can do.

A class contains fields, constructors, and methods.

- The **fields** (or **instance variables**) are the data belonging to the object.

- The **constructors** create new objects of that type. To call a constructor, use the keyword new.

- The **methods** are code to manipulate that data.

The purpose of a constructor is to make a new object in a valid state. It does this by accepting values (as parameters) and saving those values in the instance variables, and typically little else. It might do some limited computation to get the object set up properly, but that's all. Any future manipulation of the object will be done by the methods.

3.4.1 Some Useful Objects

Every Java program must have at least one class, and that class must have a public static void main(String[] args) method, which is where the program begins execution. Before we get into writing any additional classes (what I refer to as the "outer language" of Java), this section will introduce several useful predefined classes.

Java provides a large number of packages, containing a very large number of already written and tested classes. This is great, because it means a lot of good code is ready for your use; but it also means you need to learn your way around those packages. This book will help with that. For starters, there are two main packages you need to know about:

- java.lang contains the most fundamental classes, and is automatically imported into any program you write.

- java.util contains most of the data structures you will need.

3.4.1.1 String Objects

A *string* is a sequence of zero or more characters. Instead of calling a constructor, as is done with most objects, a string is created by putting characters inside double quote marks. Other than that, a string is an ordinary object. The data are the characters in the string, and there are a few dozen methods for working with that string.

For example, suppose you have

```
String language = "Java";
```

You can get the length of this string by using the length() method:

```
int numChars = language.length();
```

To send a message to an object: **Name** the object, put a **dot**, then say what **method** you want the object to execute, and what **arguments** (if any) the method needs.

I find the formal terminology awkward, so I like to say we "talk" to an object. We "tell" it something, or "ask" it something. In the above, we said, "Hey, language, what is your length?" Similarly, language.charAt(0) says, "Hey, language, what is your first character?" and language.toUpperCase () says, "Hey, language, give me an all caps version of yourself."

Unlike many objects, strings are *immutable*—they cannot be altered. Methods like toUpperCase never change the original string; they always return a new String object.

3.4.1.2 StringBuilder Objects

A more typical object is the StringBuilder. Strings are immutable, so if you make thousands of modifications to a string, you are actually creating thousands of new strings. This can be expensive. It is more efficient to use a *mutable* (modifiable) StringBuilder object.

To create a new StringBuilder object (or any other kind of object), use the keyword new, the name of the class, and any required arguments. Like this:

```
StringBuilder builder = new StringBuilder("Java");
```

StringBuilder has lots of methods for changing the string data, all of which use the standard dot notation. For example, to add text to the end, you can say

```
builder.append("Script");
```

Here are a few of the many methods you can use:

- charAt(*index*) — returns the char at the specified *index*.
- insert(*index, string*) — puts the *string* into the StringBuffer starting at the *index*.
- replace(*start, end, string*) — replaces the characters from *start* to *end*-1 with *string*.
- delete(*start, end*) — deletes the characters from *start* up to, but not including, *end*.

When you are finished, you can ask the StringBuilder object to return a String version of itself.

```
language = builder.toString(); // now "JavaScript"
```

Almost all provided classes and objects keep their data private, and the only way to access their data is by using the methods they provide. When they do make data available it is usually as a constant, for example Math.PI and Math.E in the Math class. This is good practice in general.

3.4.1.3 Using Scanner

Since it is fairly simple to produce output that the user sees, using the methods print and println, you might think it is easy to get input from the user. It isn't.

To read input from the user, first import the Scanner class.

```
import java.util.Scanner;
```

(Remember that imports go before the class declaration). Next, define an object of this type:

```
Scanner scanner = new Scanner(System.in);
```

The System.in argument says the scanner is to take input from the keyboard. (The argument could also be a file, or even a string, which is nice for testing purposes. We don't explore those options here.)

A scanner can read in either "tokens" or lines. A **token** is any sequence of characters bounded by **whitespace** (spaces, tabs, newlines), while lines are bounded by newline characters.

To read in tokens, a scanner has the methods next() (reads a token as a string), nextInt(), nextDouble(), and nextBoolean(). It also has methods for a number of other types, not including char. An Input MismatchException will result if the user enters a value of the wrong type.

One way to avoid errors is to check the type of the next token by "looking ahead" at it, with the methods hasNextInt(), hasNextDouble

(), hasNextBoolean(), or just hasNext(). Or, calls to the scanner can be made inside a try-catch statement.

The method nextLine() will read in, as a string, the next line.

> **Caution:** Tokens are delimited by whitespace, while lines are delimited by newlines; but newlines are a kind of whitespace. If a token is read at the end of a line, a following nextLine() will return an empty string.

You seldom need more than one Scanner. If you want to make use of a scanner in several different classes or packages, use a public static variable to hold the Scanner object, and put it in an accessible class.

Scanners should be closed after use: scanner.close().

As with most of the classes described in this book, the Scanner class has many more methods than are mentioned here. For example, a scanner may use regular expressions to tell it what to read.

3.4.1.4 Console
The class java.io.Console provides a much simpler way to read input from the user than the Scanner class, but it has a significant disadvantage: It requires the presence of an interactive "console." Depending on how the Java program is being executed, a console may or may not be present. In many cases, Console can be used when running from the command line, but not when running from an IDE.

The constructor call new Console() will return null if no console is available. Otherwise, here are some of the operations available on the new console:

- readLine() returns one line, as a string.
- readLine(*formatString*, *value*, ... , *value*) formats and displays a string to be used as a prompt, then reads and returns one line.
  - *Format strings* are described in section 5.2.2.10. A plain string, with no interpolated *values*, can also be used.

- `readPassword()` returns one line in a character array (that is, a `char[]`), without displaying what is typed.

- `readPassword(`*formatString,* ***value,*** *... ,* ***value****)* formats and displays a string to be used as a prompt, then reads and returns one undisplayed line in a character array. A plain string can also be used.

- `printf(`*formatString,* ***value,*** *...,* ***value****)* formats and displays a string.

- `writer()` returns a `PrintWriter` associated with this console.

  - A `Console` object does not itself have `print` and `println` methods, but these messages can be sent to the `PrintWriter` returned by `writer()`.

3.4.1.5 Objects, Generics, and Stacks

The most general type of object is `Object`. If you declare an array of `Object`, you can put any kind of object into it—strings, stacks, threads, whatever. Or you can be more specific, and declare an array of (for example) `String`, and the array can then hold only strings.

Along with arrays, Java has various types of `Collections`: `Stacks`, `Lists`, `HashMaps`, and so on. Originally, *any* type of object could be pushed onto a `Collection`, and there was no way to be more specific. When you got a value out of the collection, you got an `Object`, and had to *cast* it to the correct type. For backwards compatibility, this style is still allowed.

For example, Java has a `Stack` type (in the `java.util` package), with operations `push` and `pop` (among others).

```
Stack stuff = new Stack();
stuff.push("abracadabra");
stuff.push(new File("abc.txt"));
File foo = (File)stuff.pop();
String spell = (String)stuff.pop();
```

In modern code, it is preferable to be specific as to what type of values may be put into a stack. This is done by using ***type parameters***, or ***generics***. The type parameter is put into angle brackets after the object type.

```
Stack<String> words = new Stack<String>();
words.push("abracadabra");
words.push(new File("abc.txt")); // not legal
```

To minimize redundancy, the type parameter in the definition (that is, after the word new) can be an empty "diamond," <>.

```
Stack<String> words = new Stack<>();
```

> **Note:** In the version of Java I am using, apparently even the "diamond" can be omitted, but this is not an announced feature of Java.

As an added bonus, when you retrieve an object from a genericized collection, you no longer have to cast it to the correct type.

```
String word = words.pop();
```

The genericized type name can be used wherever an "ordinary" type name can be used, such as in the declaration of a method. For example,

```
int find(String target,
    Stack<String> words) { ... }
```

3.4.1.6 Maps

One of the most useful objects in the java.util package is the HashMap.

A *map* is a lookup table, or dictionary; it associates **keys** with **values**. For a contact list, the key might be a person's name, and the value that person's phone number.

```
HashMap<String, Integer> phones = new HashMap<>();
phones.put("Joan", 555_1212);
```

> **Note:** The above works because, although a primitive cannot be used where an object is required, Java will "wrap" the int value 555_1212 into an Integer object.

A HashMap is a particular kind of Map which supports extremely fast lookups. Any object types can be used as keys.

Note: If the *keys* are user-defined objects which have a user-defined `equals` method, then those objects *must* also have a user-defined `hashCode` method that gives equal hash codes for equal objects.

A few of the important operations on a `HashMap` are:

- *map*.`put(`*key, value*`)` — adds the *key/value* pair to the *map*, possibly replacing a previous *value*.

- *map*.`putIfAbsent(`*key, value*`)` — adds the *key/value* pair to the *map*, unless the *key* is already in it with a non-null value.

- *map*.`get(`*key*`)` — returns the value associated with the *key*, or null if the *key* isn't in the *map*.

- *map*.`getOrDefault(`*key, defaultValue*`)` — returns the value associated with the *key*, or *defaultValue* if the *key* isn't in the *map*.

- *map*.`size()` — returns the number of key/value pairs in the *map*.

- *map*.`clear()` — removes all entries from the *map*.

- *map*.`remove(`**key**`)` — deletes the *key* and its associated value from the *map*.

- *map*.`keySet()` — returns a Set "view" of all the keys in *map*.

Note: A *view* is like a "window" into the object, and changes as the object changes. In the above, the Set returned by keySet can be used just like an "ordinary" set, except that changing the contents of *map* will change the values in the set.

3.4.1.7 The Java API

The Java **API** (*Application Programmer Interface*) is a huge resource consisting of about seven thousand classes, organized into about two hundred packages. It is important to be able to find your way around this resource and make use of it.

To find the documentation, search online for "java se 17 api" or similar. One of the top hits should be something like "Overview (Java SE 17 & JDK 17)."

(If you are programming for Android or similar, you will want the Java SE 8 documentation instead.) Following that link should take you to a page with a long list of *modules*; click on the one for java.base. Bookmark this page; it is a good starting point. If you are interested in GUI development, also bookmark the link to java.desktop.

One of the packages on the java.base page, very near the top of the list, is java.lang. This package is necessary for every Java program and is automatically imported into every Java program. Click on java.lang to go to a page listing all the classes in this package.

The java.lang page contains a brief description of the purpose of the package, and very brief descriptions of what some of the classes are for. Following that is a list of "Related Packages," followed by a tabbed list of classes. For purposes of illustration, choose either "All Classes and Interfaces" from the tabbed list (probably already selected) or "Classes."

You will see some of the classes we have already mentioned, such as Character and Exception. Scroll down and click on String.

Right under **Class String** you will see that its superclass is java.lang. Object (clickable) and that it has implemented some interfaces (also clickable). The methods inherited from Object will not be described on this page (unless they have been overridden), but they will be listed further down. Methods from the interfaces are described below, along with all the other methods.

Next is a brief explanation of string objects, a field summary, a list of constructors, and further down a tabbed list of lists, one of which is "All Methods." If that tab isn't already selected, then click it.

We will pick one method on this page to examine. Scroll down to the line that looks like Table 3.1:

TABLE 3.1   Short indexOf entry in Java API

int	indexOf(String str)	Returns the index within this string of the first occurrence of the specified substring.

This line says that the indexMethod takes a String as a parameter, and returns an int result. After this, there is a brief description of what the method does—a longer description is further down the page. What is only *implied* (because this is a method in the String class) is that indexOf is a message you send to a String: For example, story.indexOf("Toby") searches the string story for the string "Toby".

In this line, indexOf and String are bold, meaning that they are clickable. Often, the description is all you need, but you can click on the method name to jump down to a detailed description.

There will be a lot on these pages you don't understand. That's fine; the important thing is to get comfortable exploring the documentation, and using the parts you do understand. If you are working a lot with strings, it is worthwhile to look through the methods to find ones you might use.

One important word to know is "deprecated." A **deprecated** method is one that still works, but has been supplanted by something newer and better. Don't use deprecated methods if you can avoid it. Usually there is a link to the newer, shinier version.

3.5 OBJECTS AND CLASSES

The syntax of classes and objects will be discussed later, but it is helpful to begin with some understanding of what these things are.

Before object-oriented programming, data and functions would be distributed throughout a program, perhaps grouped to some extent, but with no formal organization. Object-oriented programming provides that organization.

An **object** is a "thing." Some objects represent things in the real world, such as a Customer or a Date. Most objects represent things in the "computer world," such as a String or a HashMap. Some things are in-between, such as a Calendar. Each object has some data, called **fields**, describing this particular object, and it has some methods, defining what the object can do.

A *method* is a *function that belongs to an object* (or, in some cases, to a class). The methods manipulate the data of the object in various ways, such as updating it or providing information about it. Originally, Java had no actual functions; it only had methods.

A *class* defines a *type* of object. It tells what fields are in each object, and what methods operate on that object.

For example, if you were to write the software to maintain an online store, you might have:

- An Inventory object to maintain a list of Item objects you have for sale.

- Numerous Item objects, each with a price, a description, a shippingWeight, a numberOnHand, and so on.

- An Order object might be a list of Items being ordered by a Customer. You might have methods to add an Item to this order and to remove an Item from it.

- Each Customer object could have a name, a currentOrder (of type Order), an amountOwed, and so on.

Each class has at least one *constructor* for making new objects of that type. To create a new Item object, you may have to provide the constructor with a description of the item, its shipping weight, its price, and whatever else is important about the item.

> **Key concept: *Object-oriented programming*** is all about creating a society of cooperating, active "agents" (called "objects") that, working together, accomplish the desired task.

In Java almost everything, and certainly all executable code, is in classes.

An *interface* is a list of methods that a class may choose to implement. Interfaces are described in section 4.1.3 and 5.3.2; for now, it is not too misleading to think of an interface as a kind of class.

CHAPTER 4

The "Outer Language" of Java

T HE EARLIER SECTIONS OF THIS book focussed on what can be done within a single "top level" class. A typical Java program consists of multiple top-level classes, and may also use abstract classes, interfaces, any or all of the four types of inner class, as well as the specialized Enum class. While it is not standard terminology, you can think of this structure as the "outer language" of Java.

4.1 CLASS STRUCTURE

A *class* defines a type of object. It tells what data objects of that type contain and what methods they have. Here are the most important parts of a class definition:

```
access class ClassName {
    fields
    constructors
    methods
}
```

Every object has a type, and the name of that type is the same as the *ClassName*. If you define a class Item, then every object created from that class will be of type Item.

DOI: 10.1201/9781003402947-4

Normally, every top-level class goes in a separate file, and the name of the file must be the name of the class, with the extension .java.

> **Note:** More than one top-level class *can* be put in a file, but only one of them can be public, and that is the one the file must be named after. However, one class per file is the recommended organization.

4.1.1 A Simple Class

We will begin by looking at a simple example of a class; later sections will describe each of the parts of a class in detail.

The name of the class is Password, and each object created from the class will hold one password. The method matches will tell us if a password is correct, and the reset method will allow us to change it. Without further ado, here's the class:

```
public class Password {
   private String password;

   public Password(String password) {
      this.password = password;
   }
   public boolean matches(String attempt) {
      return attempt.equals(password);
   }

   boolean reset(String oldPassword,
                 String newPassword) {
      if (matches(oldPassword)) {
         password = newPassword;
      }
      return password.equals(newPassword);
   }
}
```

The name of the class is Password, and it is public, so it can be seen and used anywhere in the project.

The class has a field named password, of type String. It is private, so it cannot be seen or used outside this class.

Next in the class is a constructor. It has the same name, Password, as the class that it is in, and it will return a Password object. (Constructors do not use an explicit return statement.)

Notice that the constructor has access to *two* different variables, both named password. One is the field, or instance variable, while the other is a parameter. This may look strange, but it is quite commonly done, especially in constructors. To distinguish between them, the name password by itself refers to the parameter, while this.password refers to the instance variable.

Next is a method named matches, which will return a boolean (true or false) value. Because strings are objects, the matches method must compare them using equals.

> **Note:** Although using == to compare strings *often* works, it won't work here; see section 5.2.2.8 for an explanation. You should always use equals to compare strings.

Finally, there is a reset method that takes two strings as parameters and tells whether the reset succeeded. It is not marked public, protected, or private, so it has package access—it can be used by any class in the same package.

4.1.2 The Class Header

The class header may be as simple as the word class followed by the name of the class, or it may be as complex as the following:

access class *ClassName* extends *SuperClass*
   implements *Interface₁*, ... , *Interfaceₙ*

The *access* may be either public or omitted:

- public: Can be seen and used anywhere in the project.

- *package:* (default, no keyword) Can be seen and used by any classes in the same package (directory). The package keyword, which specifies which directory this class is in, cannot be used here.

There are two additional access types:

- `protected`: Can be seen and used by any classes in the same directory, and by any subclasses of this class, wherever they may be.

- `private`: Can be seen and used only within this one class and, if in an inner class, by its enclosing classes.

Fields and methods can be labeled with any one of the above access types, with "package" as the default. Local variables of a method cannot be so labeled; they're just local.

By convention, the **ClassName** should begin with a capital letter. It defines a *type*; every object created from this class will be of type **ClassName**.

Classes are arranged in a hierarchy, with the `Object` class at the root (top) of the hierarchy. Every class except `Object` **extends** one other class, called its **superclass**, and inherits data and methods from that superclass. If the superclass is omitted, `Object` is assumed.

Briefly, **inheritance** means that if class B extends class A, then all the data and methods in A are also part of B. B can **extend** what it receives from A by defining additional data and methods. This will be examined in detail in section 4.2.

The class may also **implement** some interfaces, as described briefly in the next section.

4.1.3 Interfaces I

An **interface** is a list of methods—just the method headers, not the body. A class that `implements` an interface must supply those methods, with the same headers but also with a body. For example, the `String` class implements the `CharSequence` interface, and that interface requires the `String` class to supply several methods, among them `charAt(index)`, `length()`, and `isEmpty()`.

A class may extend another class, thus inheriting all its fields and methods. Similarly, an interface may extend another interface, thus inheriting additional methods to be implemented.

The purpose of an interface is to provide a common set of methods used by similar classes. For example, StringBuilder (see section 3.4.1.2) also implements CharSequence, therefore it also has the methods charAt (*index*), length(), and isEmpty(), along with many others not possessed by the String class.

The syntax of interfaces will be described in section 5.3.2.

4.1.4 Fields

A class typically contains *fields* (or more accurately, *field declarations*). This is where data is kept. It is the values in these fields that make one object different from another object of the same type.

A field declaration looks like this:

static *access type fieldName* = *expression*;

If the word static is present, then there is only one copy of the variable being defined, and it is shared by all instances of the class. Otherwise, every object created from this class has its own copy of the *fieldName* variable. In the Password class mentioned earlier, every object of that type has its own password field.

> **Terminology:** An object is an *instance* of its class, so a field belonging to an object is also called an *instance variable*. A static variable belongs to the class itself, and is also called a *class variable*.

The *access* can be omitted ("package" access), or it can be either public, protected, or private.

Most fields should be marked private. Any fields that are not private can be accessed by other classes. As a program is being developed, or later updated, other classes may come to depend on these non-private variables, and this (possible) dependency makes it difficult or impossible to update or modify the class without the danger of breaking some code somewhere. Instead, all access to fields should be under the control of the methods in the class. This is how it is done in the Java-supplied classes, and how you should do it.

Note: Private fields are private *to the class, not* to the object. Objects have no privacy from other objects of the same type. For example, code in the Password class (see section 4.1.1) can access not only this.password, but also john.password, jane.password, and so on.

The *type* of a field can be the name of any primitive type (int, double, etc.) or the name of any class type (String, Exception, Password, etc.).

By convention, each *fieldName* should begin with a lowercase letter.

The *expression*, if present, is typically just a simple value, though it can be an expression involving any fields defined above it.

Examples:

```
String name;
double length = 22.75;
private int count = 0;
```

4.1.5 Constructors I

The purpose of a constructor is to create an object in a valid state. No other work should be done in a constructor.

A constructor looks a lot like a method, but the *returnType* and *methodName* are replaced by the *ClassName*. The syntax is

```
/** documentation comment */
access ClassName(parameterList) {
    declarations
    statements
}
```

In a constructor, the keyword this refers to the object being constructed.

A constructor typically doesn't declare any local variables; all it does is use its parameters to assign values to the instance variables. For convenience, it is common for the parameters to have the same names as the instance variables, so a constructor may consist of little more than some assignments of the form this.*name* = *name*;.

For example, you might have a class Customer that starts out like this:

```java
public class Customer {
    String name;
    String address;
    double amountOwed = 0;

    /** Here is the constructor */
    Customer(String name, String address) {
        this.name = name;
        this.address = address;
    }
}
```

Here, this.name and this.address refer to the instance variables, while name and address refer to the parameters.

The constructor is called with the keyword new. For example,

```java
Customer c = new Customer("Jane", "jane@aol");
```

The newly created object is returned as the value of the call to the constructor. No return statement is necessary in a constructor.

4.1.6 Defining Methods

A method is like a function, except that it belongs to a class. Like a function, it takes parameters and may return a value. The syntax is

```
/** documentation comment */
access returnType methodName(parameterList) {
    declarations
    statements
}
```

With minor exceptions, methods contain all the executable code of a program.

The optional **documentation comment** should tell the user what the method does and how to use it. It should describe any restrictions on the parameter values, and what to expect of the return value. It should *not* talk about how the method is implemented. The documentation (doc) comment may also contain **tags** to add specific kinds of information: The @param tag describes a parameter, @return describes the result, and @throws describes an exception that may be thrown. Additional tags are described in section 5.2.1.2.

The **access** tells what other classes can use this method. It can be public, "package" (default), protected, or private.

The **returnType** tells what kind of value is returned by the method. If the method does not return a value, the keyword void is required.

By convention, the **methodName** should begin with a lowercase letter. Methods may be **overloaded**; that is, there can be multiple methods with the same name, so long as they have different numbers of parameters or different parameter types. Java looks at both the name and the parameters (but *not* the return type) to decide which method to use.

Each element in the **parameterList** must be a variable **name** preceded by its **type** (for example, String password). A primitive type is passed in "by value": The method gets an independent copy of the value. An object type is passed in "by reference": The method gets a **reference** to the actual object, not a copy of it (see section 4.1.8)

If a method does not take parameters, the parentheses must still be present.

In the body of the method you can have **declarations** of variables, with or without an initial value, for example,

```
int count = 0;
```

Unlike fields, variables cannot have an **access** specifier; all variables are **local** to the method, and cannot be seen or used outside the method. Variable declarations are usually put first in the method body.

Within the method, the **statements** can refer to any fields of the class, any parameters, and any local declarations.

4.1.7 Example: Bank Account

The following (seriously oversimplified) example of a bank account class demonstrates the use of methods and the various ways that variables can be accessed.

```java
public class Account {
    private int funds = 0;

    void deposit(int amount) {
        if (amount > 0) {
            funds += amount;
        }
    }

    void withdraw(int amount) throws Exception {
        if (funds >= amount) {
            funds -= amount;
        } else {
            throw new Exception("Insufficient funds");
        }
    }

    int getBalance() {
        return funds;
    }

    void transferFrom(Account other, int amount)
            throws Exception {
        other.withdraw(amount);
        deposit(amount);
    }

    public static void main(String[] args)
            throws Exception {
        Account john = new Account();
        Account mary = new Account();
        john.deposit(100);
        mary.transferFrom(john, 75);
        System.out.println(john.getBalance());
    }
}
```

As is right and proper, all access to and modification of the field funds is handled by methods in the same class. When money is taken from a different account other, it is done by asking the other object to withdraw money.

The following line suggests one reason that fields should be private:

```
john.funds = 1_000_000;
```

Another reason is that if something unexpected were to happen to a private funds variable, the error must be somewhere within the class. If funds is not private, the error could be in any part of the program that can access this class.

The withdraw method can throw an exception. The transferFrom method could use a try-catch statement to handle the exception, but since it doesn't, it has to pass the exception on "upward." The main method does the same thing, but "upward" from here means to the operating system, which will cause the program to crash—not ideal behavior.

There are additional places where an exception can and should be thrown, for example, when withdrawing a negative amount of money.

Also worth noting is that the funds variable represents money as an *integer* amount (possibly in cents). Money should always be represented *exactly*, not approximately; using a double could lead to legal problems.

A class like this would not normally contain a main method; I put one in (temporarily) to do some very simple testing. For a much better approach to testing, see section 7.7.

4.1.8 References

In order to work with objects, it is critical to understand the concept of **references**.

Each variable in a program has a fixed, limited amount of memory in which to store its data. An int gets 4 bytes (32 bits), and a double gets 8 bytes (64 bits). The same holds true for objects: A variable of an object type (`String`, array, `Customer`, etc.) gets only 4 bytes. This obviously isn't enough for most objects.

Instead, each object is stored in a particular area of memory called the *heap*, where it can occupy as many bytes as it needs. What is actually stored in the variable is a *reference* to that location in the heap, typically implemented as a memory address.

> **Note:** A reference is similar to a *pointer* in other languages. The main difference is that arithmetic cannot be done on references.

When a primitive value is copied from one variable into another, it is duplicated. Each variable has its own copy of the value (see Figure 4.1).

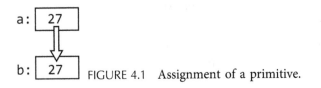

FIGURE 4.1 Assignment of a primitive.

After the assignment b = a, the variable b has a *copy* of the value from a, and either variable can be modified independently.

When an object is copied from one variable into another, it is again a simple value that is copied; but that value is a *reference* to an object, not the object itself (see Figure 4.2).

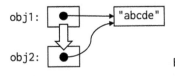

FIGURE 4.2 Assignment of an object.

After the assignment obj2 = obj1, both variables refer to the *same* object. Either reference can be used to "talk to" and change the object, and the data in the object will be the same regardless of which reference is used to view it.

The same thing happens when a method is called. If a primitive value is given as an argument, the method gets a *copy* of that value, but if an object is given as an argument, the method gets a copy of that *reference*.

It is seldom necessary to make a copy of an object, and there is no built-in, easy way to do it. If a copy must be made, probably the best way is to add a **copy constructor** in the class definition. A copy constructor is a constructor that takes an object of the same type as its parameter, and copies all the data values from it into the new object. This must be done carefully, because some of the fields of the copied object may be themselves references to other objects.

4.1.9 Constructors II

When an object is constructed, it is actually constructed in layers, with Object being the foundation layer for every object.

If you have a Customer class, and this class extends Person, and Person extends Object, then when you create a new Customer object, here's what happens:

- The constructor for Customer calls the constructor for Person.
  - The constructor for Person calls the constructor for Object.
    - The constructor for Object creates and returns a basic object.
  - The constructor for Person adds the data and methods needed for a Person object, and returns it.
- The constructor for Customer adds the data and methods needed for a Customer object, and returns it.

The result is that the Customer object *inherits* all the data and methods from Person, and all the data and methods from Object. It can use these things just as if they were defined here in the Customer class.

The first action in any constructor *must be* to call a constructor for its superclass. You can write an explicit call like this: super(*parameters*);. A call like this must be the very first line in your constructor because the foundation must be built before you can begin adding to it.

If you don't explicitly call a constructor for the superclass, Java supplies an implicit ("invisible") call for you. If you could see it, it would look like this: super();.

> **Trap:** Java provides an invisible constructor with no parameters *if and only if* you don't write a constructor for the class. Other code could depend on that invisible constructor. If you later write an explicit constructor, the invisible constructor will disappear, probably resulting in errors in previously working code.

If the Person class has an explicit constructor that takes parameters, and you write Customer as a subclass of Person, you *must* write a constructor that calls the Person constructor with the proper arguments.

```
public class Customer extends Person {
    private double amountOwed = 0;
    private String otherInfo;

    /** Here is the constructor */
    Customer(String name, String address,
            String otherInfo) {
        super(name, address); // required
        this.otherInfo = otherInfo;
    }
}
```

In this example, Customer objects have the instance variables name and address because they are inherited from the Person class. These variables should not be declared again in the Customer class.

You can have multiple constructors for a class, distinguished by the number and/or types of the parameters. Each constructor can be independent of the others. Often, however, one of these constructors does most of the work, and you would like the other constructors to call it. You can do this by using the keyword this instead of super.

If, in a constructor, you say this(*parameters*) as the very first action, then that other constructor will be called, and *it* is responsible for calling the superclass constructor. Constructors can be "chained" in this way, and only the last constructor in the chain will call the superclass constructor.

4.1.10 Static

An object bundles together data about a thing, and methods to operate on that thing. But objects are defined by classes, and a class may have its own data and methods.

> **Terminology:** A *class variable* is a variable (field) that belongs to the class itself. A *class method* is one that is not associated with any particular object. These are indicated by the word static in their declaration.

There is only one copy of each static variable, shared by all objects of that class. Static variables are used to say something about the class or something that is the same for every object in the class.

> *access* static *type fieldName* = *expression*;
> *access* static *returnType methodName*(*parameterList*) { ... }

Suppose you had a Customer class, and each Customer object holds information about that particular customer. Now suppose you wanted to keep track of *how many* customers you have; that is, how many times a Customer object has been created. You can add a howMany field to the class, but it doesn't make sense for every Customer object to have its own (possibly different) value for howMany. The solution is to add a howMany field, but make it static.

```
public class Customer {
    private String name;
    private String address;
    private double amountOwed = 0;
    private static int howMany = 0;

    Customer(String name, String address) {
        this.name = name;
        this.address = address;
```

```
    howMany += 1;
  }
}
```

Now, since howMany is a class variable, we don't need a particular object to call it; we can say Customer.howMany.

> **Note:** We don't *need* an object of the class to use its static fields and methods, but if we have one, we can use it. That is, if richGuy is a Customer object, we can say richGuy.howMany and get the same result as Customer.howMany, or the same as poorGuy.howMany. This can seem confusing because it is sending a message to a particular object, but getting a response from the object's class.

Static methods (another name for class methods) work the same way; they are attached to the class, not to particular objects. We can "talk" (send a message) to the class directly, or indirectly by talking to any object of that class. For example,

```
static int getHowMany() {
   return howMany;
}
...
int customers;
// All of the following lines are equivalent
customers = Customer.getHowMany();
customers = richGuy.getHowMany();
customers = poorGuy.getHowMany();
```

Static methods do not belong to any particular object (instance), so they cannot use instance variables or instance methods; they can only use static variables and static methods. If a static method has access to an object, however, it can "talk to" (send messages to) that object, and it can use dot notation to directly access any non-private fields of that object.

Methods that don't depend on *anything* in the class, but are in it simply because every method has to be *somewhere*, should also be made static.

```
static double feetToMiles(double feet) {
   return feet / 5280.0;
}
```

4.1.11 Escaping Static

Java is **object-oriented**, not "class-oriented." That is, objects are used a lot, and classes are used almost entirely for defining and creating objects.

However, a Java program always begins in a "static context," the `public static void main(String[] args)` method. Because it is static, it cannot use instance variables or instance methods (which belong to some object, or "instance").

If what you want to do is simple enough, you might want to just write one class with a handful of methods. In that case, you can make every method and field static, but this gets annoying in a hurry. Alternatively, you can create one object of the class that you are in, and call a non-static method on that object. That is what we did very early in this book.

```
public class MyClass {
   public static void main(String[] args) {
      new MyClass().run();
   }
   void run() {
      System.out.println("Hello World");
   }
}
```

This program starts, as does every Java program, in the static method `main`. Then it creates a new `MyClass` object and immediately calls that object's run method. Now everything else can proceed from the run method, and you are no longer forced to make everything static. (I used the name "run" for this method, but you can name it whatever you like.)

4.1.12 The Main Method

We are now in a position to explain the absurdly complex `main` method. It looks like this:

```
public class MyClass {
  public static void main(String[] args) { ... }
```

The name of the class is MyClass, so it must be in a file named MyClass.java. Compiling it results in a new file, MyClass.class, which is ready to execute. From your favorite operating system, you or your IDE tries to execute this file. How?

- public: The class and the method must both be public, that is, available from anywhere. In particular, it has to be available to your operating system.

- static: Compiling the program defines the class MyClass (and any other classes in your program), but there are no objects yet, just classes. Since there are no objects, neither are there any instance methods. But the main method is static and it belongs to the class MyClass, which does already exist. Therefore, the operating system can send the message main to the class MyClass.

- void: The main method does not return a result.

- main: The operating system always starts a Java program by sending it the message main(*arguments*). Specifically, since it is trying to run a program on the file named MyClass.class (compiled from MyClass.java), it sends the message main to the class MyClass.

  - More than one class can have a main method, so you can have more than one possible starting point in a program. For example, you might have one program to both encode and decode messages and have a main method in both an Encoder class and a Decoder class.

- (String[] args): The main method can take arguments, either from the command line or from the IDE. Arguments are separated by spaces, and come in as **strings**. It's okay if there are no arguments—zero-length arrays are legal in Java.

As an example of one of the simplest Java programs you can have, suppose you have the following program on a file named MyClass.java in a folder named myPackage:

```
package myPackage;

public class MyClass {
  public static void main(String[] args) {
    System.out.println(args[0] + args[1]);
  }
}
```

If you are in a folder/directory containing the folder myPackage, you can compile this program with:

```
javac myPackage/MyClass.java
```

You can run it by saying:

```
java myPackage/MyClass abc 123
```

And the result will be:

```
abc123
```

4.1.13 A More Complete Example

The following is a complete, if rather pointless, example of a program that uses classes and objects.

This code is in a file named Counter.java, in a folder (directory) named tools. The names of folders and files must exactly match the names of packages and classes. (Your IDE will take care of this for you.) There may be, and probably are, other classes in this same package/folder.

```
package tools;
/**
 * A simple counter class
 */
public class Counter {
  private int count; // a field

  /** Constructor to make a Counter
   * object with an initial value.
   */
```

```
   public Counter(int initial) {
      count = initial;
   }
   /** increments the counter by n. */
   public void bump(int n) {
      count += n;
   }
   /** increments the counter by 1. */
   public void bump() {
      bump(1);
   }

   /** returns the value of the counter. */
   public int getCount() {
      return count;
   }
}
```

The class describes a new type, the Counter type.

The class has one field, int count. Every object made from this class will have its own count field, so you can have multiple counters keeping track of different values. The constructor takes a parameter initial to use as the initial value of count.

The class has three methods, two named bump and one named getCount. These are declared public so they can be used from outside the package. The bump() method adds 1 to the count field, while the bump(int n) method adds n to the count field; neither returns a value. The getCount method returns the current value of count.

To complete the example, let's write a program to test our Counter class.

```
   package toolUser;
   import tools.*;

   public class CounterTest {
      public static void main(String[] args) {
         Counter c1 = new Counter(0);
         Counter c2 = new Counter(100);
```

```
      c1.bump(2);
      c1.bump(8);
      c2.bump(100);
      c2.bump();
      System.out.println(c1.getCount() + ", " +
                         c2.getCount());
   }
}
```

This class is in a separate folder, named toolUser. The second line says to import, or make available, everything in the tools package.

The package and import statements go at the beginning of the file, before the class definition.

The next line declares a class CounterTest, which is public so that it can be used by classes in different packages.

The class CounterTest contains a public static void main method, so this is where the program will begin execution.

The next lines declare variables c1 and c2 of type Counter, create new Counter objects with different initial values, and assign them to the variables.

The following lines use *dot notation* to send several bump messages, with different parameters, to the c1 and c2 objects.

Finally, the println statement asks each of c1 and c2 to fetch their value, and prints "10, 201" as the result.

4.2 INHERITANCE

Classes form a treelike **hierarchy**, with Object at the root. Every class, except Object, has one and only one *immediate superclass*, and that class has its own immediate superclass, and so on all the way up to Object at the root; all of these are *superclasses* of the class. The keyword extends denotes the immediate superclass.

When you define a class you can specify its superclass. If you don't specify a superclass, Object is assumed. Thus, the following are equivalent:

```
class Person { … }
class Person extends Object { … }
```

Classes **inherit** all the fields and all the methods of their superclasses. Every class has not only its own fields and methods but also every field and every method available to all of its superclasses. Hence, a class may contain much more information than is obvious from the class definition.

For example, if you have a Person class that has a name field, and you write a Customer class that extends Person, then every Customer object also has a name field. If your Person class has a visit method, then every Customer object also has a visit method.

Inherited methods can be **overridden** (replaced) by declaring a method with the same name and the same number and types of parameters; see section 4.4 for more details.

Constructors are *not* inherited.

4.3 CASTING OBJECTS

Recall that numeric values can be **cast** (converted) from one type to another. An int value can be put into a double variable with no trouble because a double is in some sense "wider" than an int. But to put a double value into an int variable, it must be explicitly cast to an int by putting (int) in front of the variable; for example, int pi = (int) Math.PI;.

Smartly, objects of one type can be put into a variable of a different type if and only if one of the types is an ancestor (superclass) of the other. **Upcasting** is casting to an ancestor type, and can happen automatically; **downcasting** is casting to a descendant type, and an explicit cast is required. For example, if BirthdayCake extends Cake and Cake extends Object, then the following assignments are possible:

```
BirthdayCake myCake = new BirthdayCake();
Cake cake = myCake;
Object obj = myCake;
```

```
myCake = (BirthdayCake)cake;
myCake = (BirthdayCake)obj;
cake = (Cake)obj;
```

The usual reason for upcasting is to put an object into a collection of more general objects; for example, to put a birthday cake into an array of cakes. The birthday cake does not lose its special features (candles, for example), but those features are unavailable from a variable of the more general type Cake.

When downcasting an object, Java inserts an implicit check that the object really is an object of the intended type, and throws a ClassCastException if it is not. When the object is in a variable of the more specific type, the added features (fields and methods) are again available.

You can test if an object is of a given type or supertype with the instanceof operator.

```
myCake instanceof BirthdayCake // true
myCake instanceof Cake // true
myCake instanceof Object // true
```

An instanceof test can be used to test whether a variable can be cast to a certain type, but it doesn't perform the cast.

```
if (obj instanceof BirthdayCake) {
    BirthdayCake bc = (BirthdayCake) obj;
    ... use bc here
}
```

Starting with Java 14, this can be abbreviated as

```
if (obj instanceof BirthdayCake bc) {
    ...use bc here
}
```

4.4 OVERRIDING

Objects inherit methods from their superclasses, and Object is the root superclass of all objects, therefore every object inherits all the methods defined in the Object class.

If an inherited method is not exactly what is desired, it can be **overridden** (replaced) by a different method with the same name and the same number and types of parameters. To do this,

1. Write the annotation @Override directly before the method.

   - An **annotation** is an instruction to the compiler. The @ Override annotation asks the compiler to check that the name and parameter list match with those of an inherited method because, if they don't, you are simply defining another method, not overriding one.

2. Write a method with the same name, same number of parameters, and same types of parameters (in the same order) as the method you wish to override.

   - The parameter *names* don't have to be the same, and the overriding method may even have a different return type.

3. Make sure the new method *is at least as public* as the method it overrides. (The sequence is private, "package," protected, and public.) If the inherited method is public, any method that overrides it must also be public.

It is usually a good idea, when defining your own objects, to override three of the methods inherited from Object:

- toString() returns a String representation of this object.
- equals(*obj*) tests if this object is equal to object *obj*.
- hashCode() returns an int hash code for this object.

The inherited versions of these methods are fairly useless; they exist so that they can be overridden. By defining them in Object, Java can be sure that every object has some version of these methods.

If your class overrides an inherited method, that inherited method is still available to you: just prefix the method call with super. That is, super.*methodName*(*parameters*) will ignore the local method *methodName* and use the inherited version.

An inherited field can be **shadowed** (hidden) by declaring a field with the same name. This is usually done because the programmer did not realize the field already exists; and if the shadowed field is never needed, the mistake is harmless. When a variable is shadowed, super.*fieldName* gives access to the inherited field.

4.4.1 Overriding toString

Every object has a toString method, inherited from Object. It is called automatically when "adding" an object to a string and when trying to print an object. You can also call it directly.

The inherited toString method is pretty useless. It's there primarily as a placeholder so that you can override it with a more useful version.

Here is a possible toString method for the Counter object:

```
@Override
public String toString() {
    return "My count is " + count;
}
```

The inherited toString method is public, therefore the version that overrides it must be public.

The inherited toString takes no parameters and returns a String result, so the version that overrides it must do the same.

If any of these aspects do *not* match the inherited toString method, you may have a valid method that overloads but doesn't override the inherited one. If the method is annotated with @Override, this kind of error will be caught.

While a toString method can be used to present information to the user, other methods are usually written for that purpose. The real value of toString comes during debugging when it can show the actual contents of objects.

4.4.2 Overriding Equals

Every object inherits an equals method from Object, but what that method actually tests for is *identity*. According to this method, two objects are "equal" if and only if they are the *same* object, occupying the *same* location in memory. This is also what the == comparison operator does when applied to objects.

> **Important:** For objects, == is always an identity test, not an equality test. The equals method is *also* an identity test, unless it has been overridden for that particular class of objects.

Continuing to use our Counter class as an example, here is what a typical equals method would look like:

```java
@Override
public boolean equals(Object obj) {
    if (obj == this) return true;
    if (! (obj instanceof Counter)) return false;
    Counter that = (Counter)obj;
    return this.count == that.count;
}
```

1. First, we say that we are overriding some method, then we give it the exact same header as the method we are trying to override. (The parameter obj may have a different name, but everything else must be the same.)

2. An extremely common error is to specify the *wrong type of parameter*. We normally want to compare this Counter to another Counter, so it makes sense for equals to use a Counter parameter. However, this doesn't work. To override a method that has an Object parameter, the parameter *must* be of type Object. If it isn't, the method may be legal, but it will not override equals.

3. Next we see if we are comparing the Counter object to itself. The keyword this refers to the object currently executing the method; that is, if we were testing c1.equals(c2), the word this refers to c1. The == operator tests for identity; it isn't necessary here, but it's a very fast test for a common situation.

4. Since the method will take *any* kind of object as a parameter, we probably want to return false if the method is called with an Octopus instead of a Counter.

5. If we get past the tests, *we* know that the parameter obj holds a Counter object, but the type of the *variable* obj is still Object. It would be an error to say obj.count, because not all objects have a count field. We have to *cast* obj to a Counter object and save it in a variable of type Counter in order to use it. (I like to use the variable name that, but almost any other name would do.)

6. Finally, we have two Counter objects that we can compare. This test could be quite complex, but for our simple Counter objects we'll just test if their count fields are equal.

The equals method should define an **equivalence relation**. That is, it should have the following three properties for any objects obj_1 and obj_2:

- **Reflexive:** obj_1.equals(obj_1) should always be true.
- **Symmetric:** obj_1.equals(obj_2) should always give the same result as obj_2.equals(obj_1).
- **Transitive:** If obj_1.equals(obj_2) and obj_2.equals(obj_3), then it should be the case that obj_1.equals(obj_3).

Unfortunately, symmetry can only be "mostly" achieved. If obj_1 is an object but obj_2 is null, then obj_1.equals(obj_2) should give false, but obj_2.equals(obj_1) would result in a NullPointerException. Symmetry *could* be achieved by making both of these result in a NullPointerException, but that hardly seems useful.

Fortunately, any reasonable definition of equals is likely to satisfy these properties, insofar as they can be satisfied in Java.

4.4.3 Overriding HashCode

There is a "rule" in Java that if you override equals, you should also override hashCode.

A **hash code** is an arbitrary integer assigned to an object. It has no more meaning than, say, a phone number. Hash codes are used by a number of classes, such as HashSet and HashMap. If you never use these classes, and never give your code to anyone who might, there is no need to override hashCode; but it's cheap and easy to do, so you should anyway.

The point to remember is that *equal objects must have equal hash codes*. If you use only part of an object to test for equality, use those same parts to create a hash code. This is absolutely necessary for classes like HashMap to work correctly.

It is *not*, repeat *not*, the case that unequal objects must have different hash codes. It's better if they do, but relatively harmless if they don't. If you use a hash code of zero for every object, your code may run a thousand times slower, but it will still work.

We have defined two Counter objects to be equal if they have the same count value, so the hashCode method practically writes itself.

```
@Override
public int hashCode() {
    return count;
}
```

If you have a Customer class with a name field, and if the name fields of two customers have to match for them to be considered equal, you can use the hash code of name for the hash code of your customer.

```
@Override
public int hashCode() {
    return name.hashCode();
}
```

If your equals method for Customer also requires other fields to be equal, that's okay; equal customers will still get equal hash codes. If three or four of your customers are named "John Smith," that will make no practical difference in execution times.

CHAPTER 5

Advanced Java

J AVA IS A LARGE, COMPLEX LANGUAGE. This section is "advanced" only in the sense that you don't really need to know most of this material in order to get started in the language. In fact, many of the features described here were not even present in the original version of Java; they are later additions.

5.1 INFORMATION HIDING

Information hiding—providing each section of code access to only the information it needs to know—is important in programming.

Information is not hidden for any nefarious reason; it is done to limit the amount of information a human has to deal with. Think of driving a car: It would be much more difficult if you had to pay attention to the details of timing, gear ratios, suspension, and so on. Instead, you are given easy access to only the information you need to drive.

Information hiding also reduces dependencies among code. If the internal structure of an object is not available, other classes cannot have code that depends on that structure.

In the same way, each class and each method should provide services to the code that uses them, while hiding the details of its operation.

DOI: 10.1201/9781003402947-5

5.1.1 Reasons for Privacy

Fields in an object all have package access by default; I consider this to be a design flaw in Java. Fields should be private by default. Since they are not, the programmer should mark every field private unless there is a reason to make it more public.

Here are five reasons for this statement:

1. It is the responsibility of each class to ensure the validity (consistency) of its objects, and it does not have full control if its variables are not private.

2. If a private variable in a class gets an erroneous value, the error must have been caused by something in the class, not something outside the class. This simplifies debugging.

3. If all the fields of an object are private, all manipulation of an object is centralized in the methods of that object.

4. If all fields of an object are private, the internal representation of that object can be changed without affecting any other classes. For example, the representation of points on a plane might be changed from rectangular coordinates to polar coordinates. This is not possible if other objects are already accessing the object's fields.

5. Making the fields private is a form of information hiding. It limits but also simplifies what can be done to the object in other classes.

For example, consider a class Person with an instance variable weight. Presumably, weight should never be negative. If an error occurs that causes it to become negative, and the variable is private, then we know the error must have occurred within the class Person, and nowhere else. But if weight is not private, the error could be anywhere (in, say, a Product that is guaranteed to help a person lose ten pounds a week).

5.1.2 Getters and Setters

For access to private data, **getter** and **setter** methods are often employed. These have the standardized form

access type get*Name*() and
access void set*Name*(**arg**)

The getter and setter methods for a weight variable might look like this:

```java
public int getWeight() {
    return weight;
}

public void setWeight(int weight)
        throws IllegalArgumentException {
    if (weight < 0) {
        throw new IllegalArgumentException();
    }
    this.weight = weight;
}
```

Often these methods do nothing more than get or set the value with the given *Name*, with the expectation that they may be extended later.

The use of getters and setters does incur a slight loss in performance. However, they give you the freedom to revise and update the structure of your objects without having to worry about what other classes may be accessing the fields of those objects. It also gives you a lot more flexibility. For example, your object could lie about its weight. Similarly, the getter and setter could use pounds but actually store the weight in kilograms.

```java
public double getPounds() {
    return kilograms / 2.2;
}
```

While this may seem like a lot of additional typing for minor gains in safety and flexibility, a professional IDE will create getters and setters for you with a couple of menu clicks, and you can then edit them as needed.

5.1.3 Private Constructors

If you call a constructor for a class, you *will* get an object of that class. Period. However, there may be circumstances where this is not what you want to have happen.

You may have a class that contains only static methods and variables. In that case, there is no reason ever to create an object of the class. However, if you do not supply a constructor, Java automatically supplies one for you. In this case, the solution is to supply a private constructor—it doesn't have to do anything, it just has to exist. Since you have supplied a constructor, even though it's one that nobody can use, Java doesn't supply a constructor, and no objects can be created.

Another situation is when you want only one unique object to be created. In that case, a private constructor and a public method to call it may be a good solution.

```
public class OneScanner {
    static Scanner scanner = null;
    private OneScanner() { } // constructor
    static Scanner instanceOf() {
       if (scanner == null) {
          scanner = new Scanner(System.in);
       }
       return scanner;
    }
    void close() {
       scanner.close();
       scanner = null;
    }
}
...
Scanner myScanner = OneScanner.instanceOf();
```

The same approach can be used if you want to check the parameters used for a constructor before actually constructing an object.

5.2 THE INNER LANGUAGE

5.2.1 General

5.2.1.1 Ordering
Within a class, variables and methods may be declared in any order, but the following ordering is commonly used:

- static variables

- instance variables

- static methods

- instance methods

Within a block, however, variables are available only from the point of declaration to the first closing brace.

```
{
    x = 1; // not legal here
    int x;
    x = 2; // legal here
}
x = 3; // not legal here
```

The braces around a class or interface do not form a block, but the body of a method *is* a block, so the above ordering rule applies.

5.2.1.2 Javadoc

A ***documentation comment***, or ***doc comment***, is a comment that can be used by the javadoc program to produce professional-looking documentation. This is how the official Java documentation is produced.

Doc comments should be written *for the benefit of the programmer who needs to use your code.* That programmer does not care *how* your code works, only that it *does* work. Implementation details should be put in internal comments; they do not belong here.

If your .java files are in a folder named (say) myProgram, then you can simply execute javadoc myProgram from the command line. This will produce several HTML pages which you can view in any browser.

A doc comment must begin with /**, end with */, and be placed *directly before* a class, interface, field, constructor, or method declaration. It consists of a textual description and some optional ***tags***; which tags can be used depends on the kind of thing being documented. If the documented item is genericized, the type variables can be specified with tags. Because javadoc produces HTML by default, HTML tags can be included in doc comments.

A doc comment for a **class** should provide general information about what kind of object it represents.

A doc comment for an **interface** should tell what capabilities it provides.

A doc comment for a **field** should describe the data held by the field. Most fields should be `private`; javadoc can be set to include or to ignore information about private fields and methods.

A doc comment for a constructor should tell how its parameters are used.

A doc comment for a method should tell the user what the method does and how to use it, not how it is implemented.

Doc comments may contain javadoc tags. Here are the most common ones:

- `@author` **Author name** (for classes and interfaces)

- `@version` **date or version number** (for classes and interfaces)

- `@param` **name purpose** (for describing a parameter of a method or constructor; use one tag for each parameter)

- `@param` **typeParameter purpose** (for type parameters of genericized classes, methods, and constructors; use one tag for each type parameter)

- `@return` **description** (for methods, to tell what is expected of the result)

- `@throws` **exceptionType description** (for exceptions possibly thrown by methods or constructors; use one tag for each exception type)

- @exception is a synonym for @throws

- @deprecated *text* (should tell why this class or method should no longer be used, and should suggest an alternative)

A good IDE can generate skeletal doc comments for you, so all you have to do is fill in the details.

The doc comment for a method should begin with a verb phrase, for example, "Finds the median value." In other words, write the doc comment as if it began with the words "This method … ."

> **Python programmers:** Java differs from Python style, which would be to write the doc comment as an imperative statement: "Find the median value."

Use the word this when referring to the current object, for example, "Returns the numerator of this fraction."

The @param and @return tags do not need to mention the *type* of the parameters or of the return value, because javadoc will do that.

If it is too difficult to write the doc comment for a method, or if a method is in sections separated by comments, this may be an indication that the method is trying to do too many things. A good IDE can help you break the method up into separate well-named methods, each with a single purpose.

Classes are organized into packages, with each public class on a separate file. To provide documentation that describes the entire package, you can write a file with the specific name package-info.java. This file typically consists of a documentation comment plus one line identifying the package and its location, like so:

documentation comment
package *full.path.to.packageName*;

5.2.1.3 Var Declarations

With newer versions of Java, variables declared in a method with an initial value may be specified with var rather than an explicit type. That is, instead of

```
int[] numbers = new int[100];
```

you can say

```
var numbers = new int[100];
```

This works because the type is obvious from the initial value.

The var declaration can also be used in the two kinds of for loop and in the try-with-resources statement. It cannot be used for class or instance variables (those declared within a class but not within a method).

Although var presumably is an abbreviation of "variable," it can be combined with final to declare constants.

5.2.1.4 Namespaces

Names are kept in **namespaces**, and the names in one namespace are independent of the names in other namespaces. Thus, for example, a variable may have the same name as a method without causing any conflict. Java uses six different namespaces:

- package names
- type names
- field (variable) names
- method names
- local variable names (including parameters)
- labels

In an instance method, a field name may be distinguished from a local variable name by prefixing the field name with the keyword this. Other names are assigned to namespaces according to how they are used in the code; for example, a method name is always followed by parentheses.

5.2.2 Data
5.2.2.1 Wrapper Classes
Primitive values in Java are not objects, so you can't talk to them (send a message to them) the way you would to an object. To make up for this lack, each primitive type has a corresponding **wrapper class**. Those classes are: Boolean, Byte, Character (not Char), Double, Float, Integer (not Int), Long, and Short. The wrapper classes are in java.lang, which is automatically imported into every program.

Wrapping and unwrapping happen automatically. If a method expects an Object as an argument, but you call it with a primitive, the primitive will automatically be "wrapped" into the correct kind of object. Similarly, if you try to add 1 to an Integer object, that object will be unwrapped to an int.

> **Trap:** If a and b are Integer (not int) values, the test a==b tests whether a and b are *equal* for values less than 128, but tests for *identity* (whether a and b are the same object) for larger values. The equals method, a.equals(b), tests for equality in all cases.

Each wrapper class has some useful static constants and methods. Since they are static, you use them by talking to the class, in many cases providing the primitive as an argument to a method. For example, there is a special double value named *NaN* (*Not A Number*), held in the static constant Double.NaN. If you have a double variable d and you want to know if it holds this value, you can ask Double.isNaN(d).

5.2.2.2 Integers
An int is a 32-bit integer that can hold numbers in the minus two billion to plus two billion range. If you need or want the exact limits, they are given by Integer.MIN_VALUE and Integer.MAX_VALUE.

Integers are usually written in **decimal**, using an optional sign and the digits 0 to 9.

An **octal** number is any number whose first digit is a 0. It may have an optional sign and the digits 0 to 7. For example, the number written as 0123 is the same as the decimal 83.

A **hex** or **hexadecimal** number begins with an optional sign and either 0x or 0X, followed by the digits 0 to 9 and A to F (or a to f).

To improve the readability of long numbers (decimal, octal, or hex), you can put underscores in the number, but *only* between digits: 1_000_000_000. These underscores are ignored.

To convert a String to an int:

- Integer.parseInt(*string*) — The string may begin with a plus or minus, but all remaining characters must be digits. In particular, underscores are not allowed.

- Integer.parseInt(*string*, *radix*) — Same as above, but the string need not represent a decimal number. The *radix* may be any integer between 2 and 36.

There are a number of ways to convert an integer *intValue* to a String:

- The easiest way is to "add" an empty string to it: *intValue* + "".

- Integer.toString(*intValue*) — Returns a string representation of a decimal number; a negative number will begin with a minus sign.

- Integer.toBinaryString(*intValue*) — Returns a string representation of an unsigned binary number.

- Integer.toOctalString(*intValue*) — Returns a string representation of an unsigned octal number.

- Integer.toHexString(*intValue*) — Returns a string representation of an unsigned hexadecimal number.

- Integer.toString(*intValue*, *radix*) — Returns a string representation of a number in the given *radix*, with a minus sign if *intValue* is negative. Characters used as digits are 0123456789abcdefghijklmnopqrstuvwxyz.

5.2.2.3 Doubles

A double is a 64-bit "real" (floating point) number, with an optional exponent. As with integers, a double value may contain underscores, but only between digits. The wrapper class for a double is Double.

Some useful static values from the java.lang.Double class are:

- Double.MIN_VALUE — the smallest number that can be represented as a double.

- Double.MAX_VALUE — the largest number that can be represented as a double.

- Double.MIN_EXPONENT — the smallest allowable (negative) exponent.

- Double.MAX_EXPONENT — the largest allowable exponent.

- Double.NEGATIVE_INFINITY — the result of dividing a negative number by zero.

- Double.POSITIVE_INFINITY — the result of dividing a positive number by zero.

- Double.NaN (Not A Number) — the result of dividing zero by zero, or several other meaningless operations. This is the only value that is not equal to itself. To test for it, you can use Double.isNaN(*value*).

The method Double.parseDouble(*string*) will convert a *string* representing a double number into an actual double. The *string* may contain leading and trailing whitespace, but not underscores.

5.2.2.4 Characters and Unicode

A **character encoding** is an agreed-upon mapping between characters and integers: 'A' is 65, 'B' is 66, and so on. Java uses Unicode internally, specifically UTF-16. Unicode is complicated, and a bit of history might help to make sense of it.

One of the earliest character encodings was **ASCII, American Standard Code for Information Interchange**. It used one byte per character. A byte is eight bits, but ASCII used only 7 of them because it was based on a seven-bit teleprinter code. Seven bits was enough to represent 128 characters, which seemed like enough at the time.

Unfortunately, that left one bit free, and if that extra bit were set to 1 rather than 0, another 128 characters could be added: dashes, "smart quotes," French characters, and so on. So every manufacturer did so, and did it differently, with the result that, say, smart quotes on a Windows machine came out as garbage characters on the Macintosh, and vice versa. You still see the occasional garbage character today, from people who unknowingly use some platform-specific encoding for non-ASCII characters.

Today, almost everything uses *Unicode*, which is adequate for most of the languages of the world. Unicode includes mathematical symbols, arrows, traffic signs, emojis, and more.

When Java adopted Unicode, Unicode used two bytes, 16 bits, per character. The ASCII character set is a subset of Unicode—'A' is still 65, and so on. This allowed for 65536 characters, which was enough until Chinese, Japanese, Arabic, and a few other languages were added to the mix.

> **Terminology:** In Java, a *code point* is a numerical encoding of a Unicode character that can fit in two bytes; that is, '\u0000' to '\uFFFF'. A *supplementary character* is one that requires more than two bytes. Java can handle supplementary characters, after a fashion, but most of the methods in the Character class can only work with code points.

Internally, Java represents strings using single-byte characters when it can, two-byte characters when it must, and more bytes when it has no other choice. Fortunately, it does a good job of hiding this complexity from the programmer. Character methods that take a "code point" as an argument take either an "ordinary" character or a number less than 65536.

A char is a primitive type, so it cannot be treated like an object. To make up for this lack, the java.lang package contains a Character class with many static methods. These include Character.is*X*(*char*), where is*X* is one of isDigit, isLetter, isLetterOrDigit, isLowerCase, isUpperCase, and isWhitespace. Each of these methods can take either a character or an integer as an argument.

Besides the static methods in the Character class that do things like test if a character is a digit, or test if a character is a letter in some language, there are two of some interest:

- Character.getName(*n*) — Returns the name of the Unicode character whose integer value is *n*. For example, Character.getName ('é') returns the string "LATIN SMALL LETTER E WITH ACUTE".

- Character.codePointOf(*string*) — Returns the numeric value of the character whose Unicode name is *string*. For example, given the string "LATIN SMALL LETTER E WITH ACUTE", the return value is 233, that is, (int)'é'.

5.2.2.5 Booleans

Booleans are simple. There are only two boolean values, true and false. The static method Boolean.toString(*boolean*) will return one of the two strings "true" or "false".

If you have been programming in a language that allows integers to stand in for booleans (for example, using 0 to mean "false"), that doesn't work in Java.

There is a method Boolean.parseBoolean(*string*), but it is equivalent to the simpler *string*.equals("true").

5.2.2.6 Other Primitives

Here are the other four primitive types:

- A long is a 64-bit integer that can be up to about nineteen digits (about plus or minus nine quintillion). To write a literal long value, suffix it with L. Numbers with this many digits are best written with underscores; for example, 146_603_833_310_800L.

- A short is a 16-bit integer in the range -32_768 to 32_767.

- A byte is an 8-bit integer in the range -128 to 127.

- A float is a 32-bit "real" (floating point) number with only about 8 digits of accuracy and a much smaller range of values.

These additional primitive types exist for the purpose of saving storage or, in the case of long, for dealing with very large integers.

> **Note:** For integer values too large even for long variables, there is a java.math.BigInteger class; see section 10.5 for an example that uses this class.

Numeric types are ordered from "wider" to "narrower": double, float, long, int, char, short, byte. A value of one type can be assigned to a variable of a wider type: floats to doubles, and so on.

A value of one type may not "fit" into a variable a narrower type; bits could be lost. To ensure that the programmer really means to make this assignment, Java requires an explicit *cast*. Casting does not *prevent* errors, it just allows a questionable assignment. For example, the cast (byte)250 is legal, and results in the value -6.

Most arithmetic on short or byte values is done by first promoting the values to int values, so the result is an int value that must be downcast to the proper type. For example, if sh is of type short, then instead of

```
sh = sh + 1;
```

you would need to say

```
sh = (short)(sh + 1);
```

The shorthand forms *op*= that combine arithmetic with assignment avoid the need for a cast. This is legal:

```
sh += 1;
```

5.2.2.7 Arrays
Arrays are objects, and they have a length field, but most of the methods on arrays are just those inherited from Object. However, the class java.util.Arrays provides a number of useful static methods.

- `Arrays.toString(array)`— Returns a string representation of the *array*. The *array* may be of any type.

- `Arrays.deepToString(array)`— Returns a string representation of the *array*. The *array* must be an array of objects. This is the method to use for multidimensional arrays.

- `Arrays.sort(array)`—Sorts the *array* in ascending order, and returns void. The array may be of any primitive type except `boolean`, or any object type that implements `Comparable`. (A large number of Java-supplied objects do implement `Comparable`).

- `Arrays.binarySearch(array, key)`— Searches the *sorted* *array* for the *key* and returns the index at which it is found. If the *key* isn't found, the method returns the negative index -*p*-1, where *p* is the position that the key would be, if it were in the array. The array may be numeric or any object type that implements `Comparable`, but it may not be a `boolean` array.

- `Arrays.equal(array1, array2)`— Tests whether two arrays of the same type are equal to each other. Arrays of objects are compared using that object's `equals` method.

As noted earlier, an *interface* is a list of methods that a class can choose to implement.

The `Comparable` interface requires one method, `compareTo(`*Type obj*`)`, where *Type* is the name of the class in which it is implemented. For example, if the `Person` class implements the `Comparable` interface, it must provide a method `compareTo(Person `*obj*`)`. The result returned by this method should be negative, zero, or positive according to whether this object is less than, equal to, or greater than *obj*.

If comparing on some numeric attribute of the objects (say, a person's age), the `compareTo` method can simply return `this.age - `*obj*`.age`.

5.2.2.8 Strings

`Strings` are objects. There are about fifteen constructors for strings, but the usual way to make a string is just to put some characters between double quotes. Once this is done, you can send messages to the string in the usual way.

For example, if s is a string, you can ask how many characters it has by saying s.length(). You can get an uppercase version of it by asking s.toUpperCase(). You can ask if it contains "Java" as a substring by asking s.contains("Java"). And so on, and so on.

It is useful to remember that strings are **immutable** objects. There is no message you can send to a string that will change the characters of that string. Methods like toUpperCase return a new string, but leave the original string untouched.

Strings have an equals method that you can and should use when comparing strings. If *s* and *t* are strings, you can ask *s*.equals(*t*) and get the results you expect. But there are two potential traps.

> **Trap #1.** You can't send a message to a null object. If *s* is null, *s*.equals(*t*) will result in an error. But if *t* is null and *s* isn't, the method correctly returns false. Therefore, if you are comparing a String variable to a literal string, it's better to send the equals message to the literal string, and make the variable an argument.

Strings are immutable, so if you write the same string in several places in the program, it only needs to be stored once. Java works hard to **intern** identical strings, making only one copy of that string.

> **Trap #2.** Because strings are interned, the test *s* == *t* (which for objects is a test of identity rather than equality) *almost* always works. Sometimes Java's interning strategy fails, and this test will report false for equal strings. Therefore, don't use == for strings.

5.2.2.9 Multiline Strings
A **text block**, also known as a **multiline string**, is a special syntax for writing a string literal. It first appeared in Java 13. Here is an example:

```
System.out.println("1234567");
String textBlock = """
            First line
        Middle line
            Last line
        """;
System.out.println(textBlock);
```

This example will print:

```
1234567
    First line
Middle line
    Last line
```

Whitespace is important in determining how a text block is printed. The first statement, which prints 1234567, is just to show in what columns the following lines begin.

- The text block begins with three double quotes. These double quotes *must* be the last things on that line.

- The lines keep their *relative* indentation. In this example, the first and last lines are indented four spaces relative to the middle line.

- The indentation of the leftmost line (in this example, the middle line), is determined by the position of the closing triple double quotes.

  - If the leftmost line in the text is indented more than the closing quotes, it will be indented that much in the string. In this example, the middle line starts two spaces over from the closing quotes, so it will have two spaces in front of it.

  - If the closing quotes are indented at least as much as the leftmost line, or if they are on the same line as the last line of text, then the leftmost line will not begin with spaces.

5.2.2.10 Formatter
Sometimes you want more control over printing than System.out.print and System.out.println give you. For example, you might wish to print

numbers in neat columns. The java.util.Formatter class gives you this extra control.

The basic use of a Formatter is as follows:

```
Formatter f = new Formatter();
f.format(formatString, value, ..., value);
System.out.print(f);
f.close();
```

In this code,

1. The first line creates a new Formatter object, which is used to build up a string, and saves it in variable *f*.

2. In the second line, the ***formatString*** is expected to contain ***format specifiers*** (see below). The ***value***s are substituted into the ***formatString*** according to its format specifiers, then the resultant string is added to the Formatter object *f*.

3. The third line calls the formatter's toString() method and prints the result.

4. The last line releases the resources associated with the formatter.

Here's an example:

```
Formatter f = new Formatter();
f.format("The value of %s is %7.4f", "pi", Math.PI);
f.format(" and %s is %6.4f.", "e", Math.E);
System.out.println(f);
f.close();
```

This will print out:

```
The value of pi is 3.1416 and e is 2.7183.
```

In the above example, "pi" is substituted for the %s and the value of Math.PI for the %7.4f; the number occupies 7 character positions, 4 of them after the decimal point. The next statement does almost the same thing for Math.E, but only leaves room for 6 characters.

A Formatter accumulates all the strings sent to its format method, and has a toString method that can be used by print and println statements. It should be closed when you are done with it.

If you want to format and print a single string, the printf method will do that:

```
System.out.printf(formatString, value, ... , value);
```

A format specifier has the following syntax (illegal spaces added for clarity):

% index$ flags width conversion

The optional **index$** lets you choose which value (counting from 1, not 0) to put in this place. For example, the format code %2$s says to put the second **value** in this place, as a string.

The optional **width** is the number of character positions to use. For floating point numbers, replace **width** with **totalWidth.fractionWidth** to specify the total number of character positions to use and the number of digits after the decimal point.

Here are the available flags (which are optional):

'-' left justification

'#' alternate format (for octal and hex numbers)

'0' pad with zeros instead of spaces

' ' (A space character) to add a leading space to a positive number

'+' positive numbers are preceded by a plus sign

' , ' numbers include grouping separators

' (' negative numbers are enclosed in parentheses

and a few of the possible conversions (one of which must be present):

%b boolean

%c character

%d integer

%e scientific notation

%f floating point

%s string

%tc complete date and time

%n a newline on this platform

%% the character %

There is a great deal more to the Formatter class than this. In particular, there are more than 30 conversions specified for dates and times.

5.2.2.11 Regular Expressions

A **regular expression** describes a pattern that describes some number of strings. For example, the regular expression c[aou]t describes the three words "cat," "cot," and "cut." Regular expressions can be used to test, search, and manipulate strings.

Regular expressions are highly standardized and are available in many programming languages. If you are familiar with regular expressions, this section will tell you how to use them in Java; but if not, you can still use the following methods with strings that do not contain punctuation.

Java has a java.util.regex.Pattern class, but several methods in the String class take a properly formatted string (written below as **regex**) and treat it as if it were a regular expression. These methods are:

- *string*.matches(*regex*)—Tests whether this *string* matches the *regex* pattern.

- *string*.replaceFirst(*regex, replacement*)—Returns a string in which the first substring that matches *regex* has been replaced by *replacement*.

- *string*.replaceAll(*regex, replacement*)—Returns a string in which every substring that matches *regex* has been replaced by *replacement*.

- *string*.split(*regex*)—Strings matched by *regex* act as separators; the substrings thus separated are returned in an array.

- *string*.split(*regex, limit*)— Returns an array of not more than *limit* matching substrings.

You can use these methods without knowing the syntax of regular expressions. All you need to remember is that many punctuation marks have special meanings in regular expressions, but letters, digits, and spaces do not. So any *regex* composed only of letters, digits, and spaces stands for itself.

Unfortunately, Java strings use a backslash to escape certain characters, such as \n for newline, while regular expressions use a backslash for certain *character classes*, such as \d for a digit. This makes regular expressions somewhat hard to write in Java.

To put a backslash into a string in Java, you need to double it: \\. Thus, to insert the two characters "\d" into a Java string, you must type the three characters "\\d". Other character classes can be handled similarly.

5.2.3 Collections

Java provides a large number of **collection types**, including **sets**, **lists**, **maps**, **stacks**, **queues**, and **deques**. These types all implement the java.util.Collection interface. This is a great help in learning to use these types because it means they all have many of the same methods.

> **Note:** Although arrays are undeniably collections, they predate the Collection interface and do not implement it.

Only objects, not "primitives" (numbers, characters, and booleans) can be put into a collection.

Using these collections is slightly more complex than it might appear. Many of the Collection types, including Set, List, Map, Queue, and Deque, are themselves interfaces, not classes. This means that you can declare a variable of that type, but you cannot create one; you can only create an object of an implementing class. Thus you will often see code such as

```
Set<Item> items = new HashSet<>();
```

The above code declares items to be a Set, with all the Set operations, but not any operations unique to HashSet. If at some later point another implementation is desired, such as TreeSet, then the implementation may be changed without any harm to the code that uses the items variable.

Stack, Vector, and PriorityQueue also implement the Collection interface, but they are classes, so objects of these types may be created directly.

Here is a *very* brief summary of some of the Collection types, along with a typical implementing class.

- Set, HashSet — a collection of values with no duplicates, in no particular order.

- List, ArrayList — an ordered sequence of values, possibly with duplications.

- Map, HashMap — a mapping of keys to values.

- Stack — a last in, last out data structure.

- Queue, LinkedList — a first in, last out data structure.

- PriorityQueue — a "least" (highest priority) value out first.

- Deque, ArrayDeque — values may be inserted and deleted at either end.

- Vector — a resizable, array-based sequence of values.

Here are some of the methods listed in the Collection interface, and therefore available to all objects of the above types: add(*object*), addAll (*collection*), remove(*object*), removeAll(*collection*), clear(), contains(*object*), equals(*object*), size(), and toArray().

5.2.3.1 Iterators

An **iterable object** is any object that can be stepped through. All of Java's collection types are iterable objects. This includes various kinds of lists and sets but does not include arrays.

An **iterator** is an object that can step through an iterable object, providing the elements of that object one at a time. Iterators can only be used once; they cannot be reset to start over.

Java has three kinds of iterators.

- Enumeration is outdated and will not be discussed here. Use Iterator instead.

- Iterator is an interface that can be used with any kind of collection. It provides the methods next(), hasNext(), and remove().

- ListIterator is an interface for various types of lists. It supports traversing a list both forward and backward, as well as adding, removing, or modifying list elements.

Iterators are not thread safe (see section 9.2).

The method c.iterator() will return an iterator for a collection c. The c.hasNext() method will return true if c has any remaining elements, and if it does, c.next() can be used to return the next value.

```
List list = new LinkedList();
list.add("one");
list.add("two");
list.add("three");
Iterator iter = list.iterator();
```

```
while (iter.hasNext()) {
    System.out.println(iter.next());
}
```

The method c.remove() will remove the last element returned by next from the collection. Not all collection types allow this operation.

5.2.4 Additional Operators
With the exception of the instanceof operator, Java's operators are one, two, or three non-alphabetic characters.

5.2.4.1 instanceof
The instanceof operator tests whether a given object *can* be cast to a given type, but it's up to the programmer to actually perform the cast:

```
if (obj instanceof String) {
    String s = (String)obj;
    ... use s ...
}
```

Since Java 14, these can now be combined:

```
if (obj instanceof String s) {
    ... use s ...
}
```

5.2.4.2 The Ternary Operator
Java has a **ternary operator**, which is like an if-then-else for expressions rather than for statements. That is, it can be used as an expression or as part of an expression.

The syntax is:

booleanExpression ? *valueIfTrue*: *valueIfFalse*

For example:

```
larger = a > b ? a: b;
```

or even

```
String s = "n is " + (n % 2 == 0 ? "even": "odd");
```

The **valueIfTrue** and **valueIfFalse** do not need to be the same type, but either type must be legal in the context.

Ternary expressions can be nested, but parentheses should be used to make the nesting easier to read.

5.2.4.3 Bit and Shift Operators

Any of the integer types may be treated as a sequence of bits. If i and j are integer values, then the following operations are provided:

- **~i** — inverts every bit of i, that is, changes every 0 to a 1 and every 1 to a 0. Numerically, this is the equivalent of -i - 1.

- **i & j** — "ands" the corresponding bits together. Each resultant bit is 1 if and only if both bits are 1.

- **i | j** — "ors" the corresponding bits together. Each resultant bit is 0 if and only if both bits are 0.

- **i ^ j** — "exclusive ors" the corresponding bits together. Each resultant bit is 1 if and only if the two bits are different.

- **i << j** — shifts the bits of i to the left j places. Numerically, this is the equivalent of $i * 2^j$.

- **i >> j** — shifts the bits of i to the right j places, with the leftmost bit (the sign bit) duplicated. Numerically, this is the equivalent of $i / 2^j$.

- **i >>> j** — shifts the bits of i to the right j places, with zeros coming to the left.

The shorter integer types are converted to 32-bit integers before the above operations are performed, so the result is always an `int` value.

5.2.4.4 Increment and Decrement Operators

The **increment operator**, ++, adds one to a variable. It can be used as either a prefix operator or a postfix operator, that is, either as **++x** or as **x++**.

The *decrement operator,* --, subtracts one from a variable, and can also be used as a prefix or postfix operator.

Used as a standalone statement, or as the increment (or decrement) part of a for loop, the prefix and postfix versions do the same thing. They behave differently when used as part of an expression.

The prefix versions add or subtract one to the variable *before* using it in an expression. The postfix versions add or subtract one to the variable *after* using it in an expression. This can get very confusing; the statement

```
x = x++;
```

leaves x unchanged. Don't use these operators in an expression without good reason.

5.3 THE OUTER LANGUAGE

In the earliest versions of Java, there was just one kind of class, the "top level" class that we have been discussing up to now. Modern Java has additional class types: enums, records, final classes, sealed classes, abstract classes, and four different kinds of inner classes. In addition, *modules* give an even higher level of organization to classes than just packages.

5.3.1 Generic Classes

A *generic* or *parameterized class* is one which takes one or more *type parameters* enclosed in angle brackets, < >. Within the class, a *type variable* may be used almost anywhere a type name would otherwise be used.

In section 3.4.1.5 we discussed the use of a generic class, the Stack. Generic classes were introduced in Java 5, and a number of pre-existing classes (Stack, ArrayList, HashMap, etc.) were parameterized. For backward compatibility, you can create and use objects of a parameterized class without type parameters, but the compiler will produce warning messages.

To define your own generic class, use the syntax:

```
class ClassName<TypeVariable, ... , TypeVariable> { ... }
```

A *type variable* is like an ordinary variable, except that it holds a *type* rather than a value. Type variables are usually written as single capital letters. Within the class definition, the type variables can be used in almost any place where ordinary type names can be used.

Here's an example of a genericized class:

```java
import java.util.*;

public class Box<T> {
    private List<T> contents;

    public Box() {
        contents = new ArrayList<T>();
    }

    public void add(T thing) {
        contents.add(thing);
    }
    public T grab() {
        if (contents.size() > 0) {
        return contents.remove(0);
        }
        else return null;
    }
}
```

Now you can create a Box that can hold only a specific type of object, for example, a String.

```java
Box<String> box = new Box<String>();
```

You can use a type variable, such as T above, almost anywhere you can use the name of a type. But there are a few exceptions:

- You cannot declare static variables of a type variable: static *T thing*;

- You cannot return a type variable from a static method:
  static *T getValue*() { return *someT*; }

- You can declare, but not instantiate, an array of a type variable:
  T[] values = new *T[10]*;

- You cannot create a generic array:
  Box<T> boxes[] = new Box<T>[10];

- A generic class cannot extend (be a subclass of) Throwable.

The above code defines box to be a box of strings, so if you call box.grab
(), you know you are going to get a string (or maybe null). But within
the Box class *T* could be any type of object, so you can only use the
methods and fields defined in the Object class. If you need more than
this, you can use **bounded type parameters**.

The syntax <*T* extends *A*> "bounds" the type of T. It specifies that type
T must be either class *A* itself, or a subclass of *A*, or a class that
implements interface *A*. For example, you might say <*T* extends
Comparable>, and this would allow you to use the compareTo method of
the Comparable interface on objects of type T.

Another legal syntax is <*T* extends *A* & *B* & *C*>, where *A* is the name of a
class or interface, and the additional names are names of interfaces.

Generics do not exist in the compiled code. If you declare and use a
variable of type Box<String> and another variable of type Box<Double>,
these will be compiled separately.

5.3.2 Interfaces II

An **interface** is a list of **abstract methods**—methods that have a header,
but no body. Any class that implements the interface must supply
complete methods, with the same header (parameter names may be
different) and a body.

An interface, like a class, defines the name of a *type*. Variables of that
type can hold any object of a class that implements that type. For
example,

```
List<String> names = new ArrayList<String>();
```

In this example, List is an interface, so you cannot create objects of type List; but ArrayList is a class that implements List, so you can create objects of this type. Now you can use the methods specified in the List interface (add, remove, contains, etc.) with names. If you later decide that names should be a Stack (a class that also implements List), you can change the declaration to

```
List<String> names = new Stack<String>();
```

and no other changes in the code are required (except possibly for what you need to import).

> **Note:** Interfaces may also contain non-abstract static and default methods. Default methods can be used as is, or can be overridden in an implementing class. These features are not covered in this book.

In section 5.3.1 we defined a Box class with add and grab methods. We might later decide to write an unrelated Shelf class that also has these two methods, and then a Cabinet class, also with add and grab methods. Each of these classes might store its contents in a completely different way, possibly in a list or a two-dimensional array. The classes may also have different data and additional, unique methods.

We can write a generic interface, which we'll call Storage, to specify the methods these classes must provide.

```
interface Storage<T> {
    public void add(T thing); // no body
    public T grab(); // no body
}
```

Now each of these classes can implement the new interface, with its own versions of the add and grab methods.

```
class Box<T> implements Storage<T> { … }
class Shelf<T> implements Storage<T> { … }
class Cabinet<T> implements Storage<T> { … }
```

What this gives us is the ability to write methods that take a Storage parameter as an argument and use that parameter's add and grab methods. The interface name Storage can be used just as if it were the name of a superclass.

```
void method rearrange(Storage<T> storage) {
    // code that uses add and grab
}
```

Because rearrange works for any class that implements Storage, we don't have to write separate rearrange methods for each of the three classes Box, Shelf, and Cabinet.

The syntax for defining an interface is:

accessType interface *Name* { ... }

where the *accessType* must be either public or unspecified ("package").

An interface may contain **constants** (final variables). All variables declared within an interface are *automatically* public, static, and final, and must be assigned a value. The keywords public, static, and final can be used but would be redundant. In the same way, the methods in an interface may (redundantly) be declared with the abstract specifier.

In some interfaces, such as the Collection interface, you will find methods that are listed as "optional." This does *not* mean that an implementing class can omit these methods. Rather, it is a suggestion that the provided method can just throw an UnsupportedOperationException.

5.3.3 Abstract Classes

Suppose we want to write a method clear() to remove everything from a Box object. We might write:

```
public void clear() {
    T thing;
    do {
        thing = grab();
    } while (thing != null);
}
```

This could go in the Box class, but what if we want to use it for other Storage types? If we put it in the Box class, then it only works for Box objects. We certainly don't want to put identical copies of this method in all the classes that can use it.

One solution is to change the Storage *interface* into an ***abstract class***.

```
abstract class Storage<T> {
    public abstract void add(T thing); // no body
    public abstract T grab(); // no body
    public void clear() {
      T thing;
      do {
          thing = grab();
      } while (thing != null);
  }
}
```

An abstract class is one that may contain abstract methods, each of which must be marked with the keyword abstract. An abstract class is an intermediate between a class (in which all methods are fully defined) and an interface (in which no methods are fully defined).

With this change the Box, Shelf, and Cabinet classes no longer *implement* the interface Storage, they *extend* the abstract class Storage.

```
class Box<T> extends Storage<T> { ... }
class Shelf<T> extends Storage<T> { ... }
class Cabinet<T> extends Storage<T> { ... }
```

Because abstract classes are "incomplete" (they are missing some method implementations), you cannot create objects directly from such classes. Abstract classes exist in order to be subclassed, and the subclasses can provide the missing method definitions.

To prevent a class from being instantiated directly, but only through subclasses, a class may be declared abstract even if it doesn't contain any abstract methods.

5.3.4 Final and Sealed Classes

As noted earlier, a variable may be final, meaning that its value cannot be changed. Similarly, a *final method* cannot be overridden in any subclass, while a *final class* cannot be subclassed.

```
public final class Human {
    final String species = "Homo sapiens";
    final String getSpecies() {
        return species;
    }
    // other methods …
}
```

Interfaces *cannot* be final, since the whole point of an interface is to allow classes to implement it.

Starting with Java 16, a class may be sealed, which means that the class definition specifies exactly which subclasses it has. (A class with no subclasses cannot be sealed, but it can be final.)

```
public sealed class Thing
    permits Animal, Vegetable, Mineral { … }
```

The three subclasses must be in the same package or module as the Thing class. As a convenience, if all the subclasses are in the same *file* as the sealed class, then the permits clause can be omitted.

All subclasses of a sealed class must be either final, sealed, or non-sealed. A final class cannot have subclasses; a sealed class must have exactly the subclasses listed; and a non-sealed class may or may not have subclasses.

```
final class Animal extends Thing { … }

sealed class Vegetable extends Thing
    permits Carrot { … }
final class Carrot extends Vegetable { … }

non-sealed class Mineral extends Thing { … }
class Quartz extends Mineral { … }
```

Interfaces may also be sealed; the permits clause lists the classes that are permitted to implement it. Interfaces may be implemented by classes and records, or extended by other classes. Aside from replacing the word class with the word interface, the syntax and requirements are the same.

5.3.5 Inner Classes

Originally, all classes in Java were "top-level" classes, that is, not defined within another class. Java has since acquired four types of inner classes— member, static member, local inner, and anonymous inner.

5.3.5.1 Member Classes

A **member class** is one that is defined within another class, as a component of that class. It may have the same access modifiers as variables (public, protected, package, static, final). Aside from its location, which makes it local to the enclosing class, a member class can be used just like a top-level class.

Variables and methods defined in a class are available throughout that class. This is still the case inside the inner class; the code of a member class has full access to the variables and methods of the containing class.

```
public class OuterClass {
    int outerVariable = 0;
    public OuterClass(int number) { // constructor
        outerVariable = number;
    }

    class MemberClass {
        int innerVariable = 20;

        int getSum(int parameter) {
            return outerVariable + innerVariable +
                parameter;
        }
    }

    public static void main(String[] args) {
        OuterClass outer = new OuterClass(100);
        MemberClass inner = outer.new MemberClass();
        System.out.println(inner.getSum(3));
```

```
    outer.run();
  }
  void run() {
  MemberClass localInner = new MemberClass();
  System.out.println(localInner.getSum(4));
  }
}
```

When the main method runs, the results will be 123 and 124.

5.3.5.2 Static Member Classes

A **static member class** is defined like a member class but with the keyword static. Despite its position inside another class, a static member class is actually an "outer" class—it has no special access to names in its containing class.

To refer to the static inner class from a class outside the containing class, use the syntax ***OuterClassName.InnerClassName***.

A static member class may contain static fields and methods.

```
public class OuterClass {
    int outerVariable = 100;
    static int staticOuterVariable = 200;

    static class StaticMemberClass {
      int innerVariable = 20;

      int getSum(int parameter) {
        // Cannot access outerVariable here
        return innerVariable +
            staticOuterVariable + parameter;
      }
    }

    public static void main(String[] args) {
      OuterClass outer = new OuterClass();
      StaticMemberClass inner =
        new StaticMemberClass();
      System.out.println(inner.getSum(3));
```

```
    outer.run();
  }
  void run() {
    StaticMemberClass localInner =
    new StaticMemberClass();
    System.out.println(localInner.getSum(5));
  }
}
```

When the main method runs, the results will be 223 and 225.

5.3.5.3 Local Inner Classes

A *local inner class* is defined within a method, and the usual scope rules apply to it. It is only accessible within that method, therefore access restrictions (public, protected, package) do not apply. However, because objects (and their methods) created from this class may persist after the method returns, a local inner class is not allowed to use parameters or non-final local variables of the method.

```
public class OuterClass {
    int outerVariable = 10000;
    static int staticOuterVariable = 2000;

    public static void main(String[] args) {
        OuterClass outer = new OuterClass();
        System.out.println(outer.run());
    }
    Object run() {
        int localVariable = 666;
        final int finalLocalVariable = 300;

        class LocalClass {
            int innerVariable = 40;

        int getSum(int parameter) {
            // Cannot access localVariable here
            return outerVariable +
                staticOuterVariable +
                finalLocalVariable +
                innerVariable + parameter;
        }
```

```
        @Override
        public String toString() {
          return "I'm an instance of LocalClass";
          }
        }

        LocalClass local = new LocalClass();
        System.out.println(local.getSum(5));
        return local;
      }
   }
```

When the main method runs, the results will be 12345 (printed from the run method) and "I'm an instance of LocalClass" (printed from the main method).

5.3.5.4 Anonymous Inner Classes

An **anonymous inner class** is one that is declared and used to create exactly one object (typically as a parameter to a method), all within a single statement.

An anonymous inner class may extend a class:

new **SuperClass**(*parameters*) { *class body* }

Here, **SuperClass** is not the name of the class being defined (that class has no name), but rather the name of the class being extended. The **parameters** are the parameters to a constructor for that superclass.

Alternatively, an anonymous inner class may implement an interface:

new **Interface**( ) { *interface body* }

Inner classes are frequently used as event listeners. The example below uses an anonymous inner class (ActionListener) as a button listener.

```
import java.awt.event.ActionEvent;
import java.awt.event.ActionListener;
import javax.swing.*;
```

```
public class OuterClass extends JFrame {

    public static void main(String[] args) {
        OuterClass outer = new OuterClass();
        JButton button =
            new JButton("Don't click me!");
        button.addActionListener(
            new ActionListener() {
                public void actionPerformed(
                    ActionEvent event) {
                        System.out.println("Ouch!");
                }
        });
        outer.add(button);
        outer.pack();
        outer.setVisible(true);
    }
}
```

Because anonymous inner classes occur within a method, they break up the flow and add several lines to the method. Consequently, the actual code within an anonymous inner class should be kept very short.

5.3.6 Enums

An enum (enumeration) is a kind of class. It has a superclass, Enum, from which it inherits some methods. An enum has all the features of an "ordinary" class (fields, constructors, methods, etc.), except that an enum has a fixed, finite number of instances (objects) of the class, defined directly within the class itself. In other words, when you define an enum, you also define all its possible values, and you cannot later create additional values.

An enum is appropriate when you need a variable that represents one of a fixed set of values—for example, the months of a year. They provide type safety: You cannot, for instance, assign a Coin value to a Month variable.

The simplest form of enum consists of a list of constants, each of which is one of the values of the enum. For example,

```
enum Weekday { SUN, MON, TUE, WED, THU, FRI, SAT }
```

This example defines the type Weekday and seven instances (values) of that type. Each of these is a unique constant. Because they are unique, it is okay to compare them with == as well as with the equals method.

In the Weekday example, each of the instances (SUN, MON, etc.) has been created by (implicitly) calling the default Weekday constructor. As with any class, you can write your own constructors; however, (1) those constructors will be private, and (2) you call them, not by saying new, but by giving the instance name followed by a parameter list. For example,

```java
public enum Coin {
    private final int value;
    PENNY(1), NICKEL(5), DIME(10), QUARTER(25);
    Coin(int value) { this.value = value; }
    public int value() { return value; }
}
```

In the above,

- value is a field. It is a constant, but it can be a different constant for each instance of the enum.

- PENNY(1), NICKEL(5), and so on, are constants, created by calls to the constructor. They must precede constructors and methods in the enum.

- Coin(int value) is a private constructor that assigns a number to the value field.

- value() is an ordinary method.

Some inherited methods you can use with enumerations are:

- boolean equals(Object *obj*) tests if this enum object is equal to *obj*.

- String toString() returns the printable name of this object, for example, "PENNY".

- int ordinal() returns the position of this object in the enumeration (starting from 0).

- static *EnumType* valueOf(String *name*) returns the object whose printable name is *name*.

- static *EnumType*[] values() returns an array of all instances of this *EnumType*.

5.3.7 Records

A *record* is a kind of class, available in Java since version 14. The purpose is to encapsulate a small amount of *constant* data in a full-featured class. As an example,

```
record Range(int min, int max) { }
```

The above is a complete record declaration; you don't need to put anything inside the braces (although you may if you wish).

For this declaration, the compiler will generate a complete class with:

- Two private final int fields named min and max,

- A constructor with min and max as parameters,

- The getter methods min() and max(), and

- The methods equals(*object*), hashCode(), and toString().

You can replace the default constructor with your own, using the usual syntax for constructors. Another option is to write a *compact constructor*.

```
public Range {
    assert min <= max;
}
```

A compact constructor gets its parameters from the record declaration, and automatically saves them as private final fields.

You can override any or all of the generated methods with your own, so long as they have the same signature. You can also add fields, initializers, and methods, but they must all be static.

Records may be inner classes or local to a method.

5.3.8 Serialization

A **serializable** object is one that can be converted to a sequence of bytes, usually so that it can be written to a file. To read it again, it has to be **deserialized**. This allows objects to be stored on a file for future use.

In order for an object to be serializable,

- It must implement the java.io.Serializable interface. This is a **marker interface**—one that doesn't list any methods, so none have to be defined in order to implement it.

- Every field of the object must be either serializable or **transient** (see below).

  - Strings, arrays, and "wrapped" primitives are all serializable, as are many Java-supplied objects such as HashMap. Check the Java documentation if you are unsure.

  - A field of the object is considered serializable if it is an object that has an accessible no-argument constructor to initialize its fields when it is deserialized.

  - To keep a field from being serialized, mark it as transient. This is useful to keep sensitive information from being stored or sent across a network. It is also sometimes used for fields whose value is derived from other fields. Upon deserialization, transient fields are given a default value.

Here's the basic approach to writing out an object.

```
FileOutputStream file = new FileOutputStream(pathToFile);
ObjectOutputStream stream = new ObjectOutputStream(file);
stream.writeObject(object);
```

To read in a serialized object, the exact same classes used by the object must be present. Here's the basic approach to reading in an object.

```
FileInputStream file = new FileInputStream(pathToFile);
ObjectInputStream stream = new ObjectInputStream(file);
object = (type) stream.readObject();
```

These methods can throw an IOException or a ClassNotFoundException, so these must be handled, and the **stream** and **file** should be closed after use.

If the definitions of the relevant classes change after serialization, the deserialized results can be incorrect. To ensure consistency, the serializable class should have a **version number** associated with it.

```
access static final long serialVersionUID = longValue;
```

5.3.9 Modules

A **package** is a collection of related classes. A very large program, however, may consist of hundreds of packages. To make a class in one package available to a class in another package, it had to be made public, which makes it available everywhere. This isn't generally desirable.

Java 9 introduced **modules**, which provide additional restrictions on visibility. A module is a directory containing any number of packages, along with a top-level file named module-info.java. This file contains the text:

```
module moduleName {
    directives
}
```

where the **moduleName** must be unique, may not contain underscores, and usually has the same name as the directory it is in.

When packages are in a module, the keyword public makes an element available to other packages in the same module, not everywhere.

To use a package in one module from a package in a different module, the first module must **export** the package, and the second must **require** the package. For example, a directory named giveModule may contain packages src/com/xyz/giver and src/com/xyz/secret, along with this module-info.java file:

```
module giveModule {
  exports com.xyz.giver;
  exports com.xyz.secret to takeModule;
}
```

This specifies that the giver package can be used by anyone that requires it, while only the takeModule module can require the package secret.

> **Note:** Windows uses backslashes rather than forward slashes to indicate directory structure, while Java uses dots.

In this example, the directory containing the taker package also contains this module-info.java file:

```
module takeModule {
   requires transitive giveModule;
}
```

The optional word transitive implies that any module which requires takeModule will also have access to giveModule.

Modules may not have circular dependencies. If module A requires module B, module B cannot require module A.

All the Java-supplied packages have been organized into about 100 modules, and every module declaration automatically requires java.base. The java.base module consists of 32 packages, including java.lang, java.util, java.io, and java.math.

5.3.10 Build Tools

Java programs must be *compiled* (turned into *byte code*) before they can be executed. The javac *file* command will compile a single file (which must have the .java extension) into a file of byte code with the .class extension.

However, all but the simplest programs consist of multiple classes, each on a separate .java file. A file cannot be compiled successfully until all of the classes it depends on have been compiled. Moreover, compilation can be time-consuming, so we don't want to compile *everything* each time one little change is made. But if one Java file is changed and re-compiled, files that depend on it must also be re-compiled. Re-compiling these files may lead to re-compiling still more files.

A **build tool** takes as input a list of file dependencies, and compiles or re-compiles only those files that need it. **Ant, Maven,** and **Gradle** are popular build tools. If you are using an IDE, one or both of these tools will be built-in for you, and you can let the IDE do the work.

CHAPTER 6

Functional Programming

T HE BASIC IDEA OF *functional programming* is that functions are values, and can be treated as such. Functions can be stored in variables, passed as arguments to methods, returned as the result of a method, combined to form new functions, and applied in part or in full to arguments. Along with this is the idea that data is *immutable*; functions applied to data produce new data rather than changing existing data.

There are three factors that add to the complexity of functional programming in Java. First, Java is designed around methods, which are associated with classes; functions are a recent inclusion. Second, primitives are treated differently from objects, which leads to a combinatorial explosion of methods. Third, Java's data structures are all mutable, which is inconsistent with the general practice of functional programming.

6.1 FUNCTION LITERALS

Starting in Java 8, you can define a *lambda expression* (also called a *function literal)* as follows:

(parameters) -> expression

or

DOI: 10.1201/9781003402947-6

(parameters) -> statement

- Each of the *parameters* consists of a type (int, etc.) and a name, although in many cases, the type declaration may be omitted or replaced with var, and Java will figure out the correct type.

- If there is only one parameter, and the type is not specified, the parentheses may be omitted.

- If there are no parameters, empty parentheses, (), are required.

- The *statement* may be a compound statement (enclosed in braces) and may contain return statements.

- Functions cannot be defined at the top level; they can only be defined within methods (or within another function).

The *method reference operator*, ::, is a way of "wrapping" a method inside a functional interface, so that it can be used as if it were a function.

Essentially, *x* :: *m* is an abbreviation of *x* -> *x*.*m*(...), where *m* has an unspecified number of parameters. If there is more than one method named *m*, method resolution is performed in the usual way, by the types and number of parameters.

6.2 FUNCTIONAL INTERFACES

A *functional interface* is any interface that declares exactly one abstract method, called its **SAM** (*Single Abstract Method*). For example, the Comparable interface declares the compareTo(*T*) single abstract method, the Runnable interface declares run(), and the ActionListener interface declares actionPerformed(*actionEvent*).

The most common use of function literals is to pass them into methods as arguments. However, a method must specify the type of each of its parameters. In the case of a function literal, the type will always be the name of some kind of functional interface, but that name isn't obvious. Java provides 43 types of functional interfaces, each with an associated SAM.

For example, suppose the lambda expression is x -> x * x, and x is an integer. Then the type of this lambda expression is IntUnaryOperator, and the associated SAM is applyAsInt(*int*). As a trivial example, we can define this method:

```
void run(IntUnaryOperator fun, int n) {
  System.out.println(fun.applyAsInt(n));
}
```

When we call this method with run(x -> x * x, 12), it will print 144.

For a more interesting example, we will define a map method that applies a function to each element of an integer array and returns an integer array of the results.

```
import java.util.function.IntUnaryOperator;
import java.util.Arrays;

public class FunctionTest {

  public static void main(String[] args) {
    FunctionTest test = new FunctionTest();
    int[] a = new int[] {1, 2, 3, 4, 5};
    Mapper map = new Mapper();
    int[] b = map.apply(a, x -> x * x);
    System.out.println(Arrays.toString(b));
  }
}

@FunctionalInterface
interface ForEach {
  int[] apply(int[] a, IntUnaryOperator f);
}

class Mapper implements ForEach {
  public int[] apply(int[] a, IntUnaryOperator f) {
    int[] b = new int[a.length];
    for (int i = 0; i < a.length; i += 1) {
      b[i] = f.applyAsInt(a[i]);
    }
    return b;
  }
}
```

In this example, ForEach is a functional interface with one SAM, apply. (The annotation @FunctionalInterface is optional, but recommended because it helps Java check for errors.) The apply method is public and abstract, but we can omit these keywords because every method in an interface is automatically public and abstract.

The Mapper class implements ForEach, so it has to supply an apply method.

The main class creates an integer array a and a Mapper object map. It then calls Mapper's apply method, giving it the array a and the function x -> x * x as parameters. The result is the new array b, which is then printed.

6.3 IMPLICIT FUNCTIONAL INTERFACES

Functional interfaces don't have to be annotated with @ FunctionalInterface. Any interface that has exactly one abstract method is a functional interface.

One use for this is in programming graphical user interfaces. The ActionListener interface has one SAM, actionPerformed (ActionEvent *e*), and this is used by many user interface elements, such as javax.swing.JButton. The traditional way to associate an action with a button is something like

```
myButton.addActionListener(new ActionListener() {
  @Override
  public void actionPerformed(ActionEvent e) {
    doSomething();
}});
```

Since ActionListener is a functional interface, the above can be simplified to:

```
myButton.addActionListener(e -> doSomething());
```

6.4 PERSISTENT DATA STRUCTURES

An *immutable data structure* is one which cannot itself be changed but can be modified to produce a new data structure. For example, strings in

Java are immutable. If in addition, the new data structure shares some or all of the unmodified parts with the original data structure, it is said to be *persistent*.

For example, if a persistent hash table contains 100 entries, and one of them is changed, the new hash table may share the other 99 elements with the original hash table; but each appears to the program to be a separate, independent hash table.

"Pure" functional programming makes heavy use of persistent data structures. Java does not provide any, so this limits the value of functional programming in Java.

CHAPTER 7

Unit Testing

7.1 PHILOSOPHY

Testing is an essential part of programming. You can do *ad hoc* testing (testing whatever occurs to you at the moment), or you can build a *test suite* (a thorough set of tests that can be run at any time).

People naturally want to minimize effort, and building a test suite is additional effort. However, experiments repeatedly show that writing test suites takes less time and effort than debugging without a test suite, and results in far more reliable code. In addition, the existence of a test suite makes it *much* easier to maintain and modify the program, particularly after a few months have passed.

Besides, debugging is even less fun than writing tests.

Deadlines are often used as an excuse for not doing thorough testing— "There isn't time!" This is a flawed argument, since thorough testing *reduces* total programming time.

That said, programmers are human, and they will only do adequate testing if (1) the tests are easy to write, and even more importantly, (2) the tests are effortless to run. A good *test framework* such as JUnit makes both of these things possible.

DOI: 10.1201/9781003402947-7

It is very difficult to write tests for methods that were not written with testing in mind. To be testable:

- Methods should do only one thing, not a large variety of things. The simpler the method, the simpler the test.

- Methods should be as self-contained as possible. They should not depend on context any more than absolutely necessary. They should not require other methods to execute before this one. Tests that can be run in isolation are much easier to write than those that require elaborate setup.

- Methods should absolutely not require any interaction with the programmer. Tests that require more than a single button click to run will be run much less often, if at all.

- Methods should not do any input/output. There are advanced techniques, not covered here, for testing input/output methods without demanding programmer interaction.

Fortunately, rules for writing testable methods are also rules for a good programming style.

It is good practice to write the tests for a method concurrently with writing the method. Some even advocate writing the tests *before* writing the method, as this helps clarify what the method is supposed to do.

After a method has been written and tested, additional errors may be discovered. There is a specific technique for dealing with this situation. *First*, write a test that demonstrates the error; *then* fix it. This is useful because, for whatever reason, some errors have a habit of recurring.

7.2 WHAT TO TEST

Testing should cover both the common cases and the edge cases, where things are most likely to go wrong.

For example, if you have a method isPrime to decide whether a number is a prime, you might decide to test whether isPrime(28) is false and isPrime(29) is true. Having done that, it is probably redundant and even a bit silly to also test whether isPrime(30) is false and isPrime(31) is true.

You might, however, want to check that isPrime(15) is false, in case the method somehow decides that all odd numbers are prime. It's also worth checking worth checking that isPrime(2) is true, in case the method decides that all even numbers are non-prime. In fact, 2 is an edge case, since it is the only even prime number.

Another edge case is isPrime(1), which should be false. Although it passes the general test (not divisible by any number other than itself and 1), mathematicians define 1 as not a prime number.

Other edge cases are zero and negative numbers. Primality is not defined for these numbers, and the programmer must decide what to do in these cases (and preferably, test that that is what actually happens). If the decision is "that can't happen anyway", the appropriate thing to do is to put the statement assert n > 0; at the beginning of the isPrime method, and test that an inappropriate call throws an exception.

> **Reminder:** assert statements (see section 3.3.2.1) are "free" in that they are treated just like comments, and do not add to code size or execution time, unless they are explicitly enabled in the run-time configuration setting.

7.3 JUnit

JUnit is a well-established test framework. To use it, here's the general approach:

1. Define a class to hold the tests, and import the test framework.

2. Include any number of test methods, **annotated** (preceded) by @Test. Each test will call one or more **assertion methods**.

3. If any of the tests manipulate global variables, you should have a method annotated with @BeforeEach to initialize them.

4. Execute the class. The class does not define a main method; that is in the JUnit framework. When run, JUnit will produce a report that either (1) says all tests passed or (2) tells which tests failed.

If you have written the tests properly, they will not ask you for input or otherwise interrupt the running of the tests.

7.4 JUnit 5 Assertions

A **unit test** is a test of a single class. It is an ordinary class that imports a test framework and annotates some of its methods to mark them for special processing. First, do the following:

```
import org.junit.jupiter.api.*;
import static org.junit.jupiter.api.Assertions.*;
import static org.junit.jupiter.api.Assumptions.*;
```

The first import statement makes the annotations available, the second makes the test methods (such as assertEquals) available, and the third makes assumptions (described later) available.

Next, write the methods that will be used by JUnit. Each method should be public void, should take no parameters, and should have one of the following annotations:

- @BeforeAll annotates a static method that will be run only once before any tests are run. This is used when the tests use expensive resources; for example, it might open a database.

- @BeforeEach annotates a method that will be run before each and every test. It should reset any global variables to a pristine state so that the execution of one test does not influence the results of some other test.

- @Test marks a method as a test method. Ideally, each test method tests a single method in the class being tested. Sometimes there are several tests for the same method, testing different kinds of input. Sometimes a test method has to depend on the correct functioning of some methods in order to test other methods.

- @AfterEach annotates a method that will run after each test. This is rarely used.

- @AfterAll marks a static method that executes after all tests have been run. Its purpose is to close any resources opened by @BeforeAll.

- @DisplayName(*string*) can be put before the test class or in front of individual tests, to use *string* in place of the class name or test method name when reporting results.

The test methods (those annotated with @Test) are ordinary code but contain one or more assertions. The assertions available for use in the @Test methods include:

- assertEquals(*expected*, *actual*) compares values of any type. For comparing objects, it uses their equals method.

- assertEquals(*expected*, *actual*, *delta*) compares floating point numbers, where *delta* is the absolute amount by which the two numbers may differ and still be considered equal.

- assertArrayEquals(*array1*, *array2*) compares two arrays. For arrays of objects, this does a deep comparison. For arrays of floating point numbers, there may be an additional *delta* argument.

- assertTrue(*booleanExpression*) and assertFalse(*booleanExpression*).

- assertSame(*object1*, *object2*) and assertNotSame(*object1*, *object2*) are tests of identity, that is, whether *object1* and *object2* are references to the same object.

- assertNull(*object*) and assertNotNull(*object*).

- assertTimeout(*ms*, *function*) fails if the *function* (not method) takes longer than *ms* milliseconds.
  - Example: assertTimeout(100, () -> slowMethod(x, y));

- fail(*message*) and fail(*exception*).

All of these tests except fail may take an optional last argument *message*.

Note: The `fail` method (which, yes, causes the test to fail) is useful for writing tests that use more complex logic.

A test method may contain as many assertions as desired. However, if one fails, the remaining assertions in that method are not executed, so it is better not to have too many. Instead, write additional test methods to test different aspects of the method.

If you have a class containing a number of methods, most good IDEs will write a skeletal test class for you, so that you only have to add the assertions.

A test class may also contain unannotated methods. These are ignored by JUnit but may be used by the test methods.

7.5 TESTING EXCEPTIONS

If a method might throw an exception, you should test whether it does throw that exception when it should. However, the obvious way of writing the test does not work.

```
assertThrows(exception, methodCall); // wrong!
```

The problem is that the parameters to `assertThrows` are evaluated *before* the method is called, so if the *methodCall* throws an exception, `assertThrows` never gets a chance to catch it and deal with it.

There are two ways to solve this problem. The more convenient way, in modern Java, is for the second argument to `assertThrows` to be a *function that calls the method.* Like so:

```
assertThrows(exception, () -> methodCall);
```

This works because the function is passed to `assertThrows`, which then executes the function to cause the exception to happen. For example,

```
assertThrows(ArithmeticException.class,
             () -> divide(0, 0));
```

Note: The first argument to assertThrows must be a class, but exceptions such as ArithmeticException are *type names*, not classes. The.class suffix returns the class itself.

If you do not have functions available, the same test can be written as follows:

```
try {
    divide(0, 0);
    Assertions.fail();
}
catch (ArithmeticException e) { }
```

7.6 ASSUMPTIONS

In addition to assertions, JUnit 5 provides three kinds of *assumptions*.

- assumeTrue(*booleanExpression*)

- assumeFalse(*booleanExpression*)

If the test is not met, the test method returns without executing the remainder of the method, and the test is considered "not applicable" rather than either succeeding or failing.

- assumingThat(*booleanExpression*, *function*)

If the *booleanExpression* is true, the *function* will run; otherwise, it won't. Either way, the test method will continue.

Note: Assertions within the *function* will have no effect.

Example: assumeTrue(System.getProperty("os.name")
                        .equals("Mac OS X"));

7.7 SIMPLE TEST EXAMPLE

The following code tests a very simple class, Account, which was used as an example in section 4.1.7. It has a constructor and the methods deposit, withdraw, and getBalance (and transferFrom, which is not tested here.) The code for the Account class is not repeated here, but it can be easily inferred by looking at the test cases.

```java
package account;

import org.junit.jupiter.api.*;
import static org.junit.jupiter.api.Assertions.*;

public class AccountTest {
    Account account; // must be global

    @BeforeEach
    public void setup() {
        this.account = new Account(); // global
    }

    @Test
    public void openAnAccount() {
        assertEquals(0, account.getBalance());
    }

    @Test
    public void testDeposit() {
        account.deposit(100);
        assertEquals(100, account.getBalance());
        account.deposit(70);
        assertEquals(170, account.getBalance());;
    }

    @Test
    public void testIllegalDeposit() {
        account.deposit(-10000);
        assertEquals(0, account.getBalance());
    }

    @Test
    public void goodWithdrawal() throws Exception {
        account.deposit(100);
        account.withdraw(35);
        assertEquals(65, account.getBalance());
    }

    @Test
    @DisplayName("Exception test, old style")
    public void badWithdrawal() {
        try {
```

```
      account.withdraw(35);
      fail("Did not throw exception");
    }
    catch (Exception e) { }
  }

  @Test
  @DisplayName("Exception test, new style")
  public void badWithdrawal2() {
    assertThrows(Exception.class,
      () -> account.withdraw(35));
  }
}
```

Ideally, each method in Account should be tested individually. This isn't always feasible. In the above, money has to be added to the account before withdrawals can be tested.

CHAPTER 8

GUIs and Dialogs

A GRAPHICAL USER INTERFACE, or **GUI** (pronounced "gooey"), provides interaction with the user beyond simple text entry and printing. GUIs provide familiar buttons, text fields, menu items, and so on, common to almost all user-facing programs.

8.1 A BRIEF HISTORY

GUIs have been available from the very first Java implementation. The original GUI toolkit was the *AWT*, the **Abstract Window Toolkit**, which was platform-specific and quite primitive.

Later came *Swing*, a much better, platform-independent toolkit. It was built "on top of" AWT, and many of the AWT packages are still needed in Swing applications.

A third toolkit, *JavaFX*, was released in 2008. It was originally intended to replace Swing. While it is still available as part of the OpenJFX project, it has been dropped from the standard releases of Java. For this reason, our description of GUI programming uses Swing.

8.2 DIALOGS

A *dialog* is used to get a simple response from the user. Dialogs can be used without having to create a full-fledged GUI. To determine the location of the dialog on the screen, a *parent* component must be specified; if it is null, the dialog will be centered on the screen.

DOI: 10.1201/9781003402947-8

There are four kinds of JOptionPane dialogs: Confirm, Input, Message, and Option. Additional dialog types are provided for choosing a color (import java.awt.Color), or for loading or saving a file (various classes from java.io). You can also create your own custom dialog.

All provided dialogs are *modal*, that is, the user must respond to them before anything else can be done in the application. Custom dialogs may be modal or nonmetal.

8.2.1 Message Dialog

A *message dialog* is a modal dialog with a single OK button.

To display a JOptionPane message dialog, import javax.swing. JOptionPane and do the following:

```
JOptionPane.showMessageDialog(parent,
        "This is a message dialog.");
```

8.2.2 Confirm Dialog

A *confirm dialog* is a modal dialog with Cancel, No, and Yes buttons. The return result will be an integer equal to one of YES_OPTION, NO_OPTION, or CANCEL_OPTION.

To display a JOptionPane confirm dialog, import javax.swing. JOptionPane and do the following:

```
int yesNo = JOptionPane.showConfirmDialog(
        parent,
        "Do you really want to do that?");
if (yesNo == JOptionPane.YES_OPTION) {
    System.out.println("Action confirmed");
}
```

8.2.3 Input Dialog

An *input dialog* is a modal dialog that provides a place for the user to enter a single line of text and has Cancel and OK buttons.

To display a JOptionPane input dialog, import javax.swing.JOptionPane and do the following:

```
String userName =
  JOptionPane.showInputDialog(
    parent, "What is your name?");
```

8.2.4 Option Dialog

An ***option dialog*** is a modal dialog that displays a number of buttons, each labeled with a string taken from an array of strings. Clicking on a button returns an index into that array.

To display a JOptionPane option dialog, import javax.swing.JOptionPane and do the following:

```
Object[] options = new String[] {
  "Java", "Python", "C++"
};
int option = JOptionPane.showOptionDialog(
    parent,
    "Choose an option:",  // message
    "Option Dialog",    // title
    JOptionPane.YES_NO_OPTION,   // option type
    JOptionPane.QUESTION_MESSAGE, // message type
    null,   // icon
    options,   // array of strings or components
    options[0]); // initial selection
```

The option type may be one of DEFAULT_OPTION, YES_NO_OPTION, YES_NO_CANCEL_OPTION, or OK_CANCEL_OPTION. The message type may be one of ERROR_MESSAGE, INFORMATION_MESSAGE, WARNING_MESSAGE, QUESTION_MESSAGE, or PLAIN_MESSAGE.

If the user just closes the dialog, the integer JOptionPane.CLOSED_OPTION is returned.

8.2.5 Color Chooser Dialog

To declare and use a JColorChooser, import java.awt.Color and javax.swing.JColorChooser and do the following:

```
JColorChooser colorChooser = new JColorChooser();
Color chosenColor =
  colorChooser.showDialog(parent,
                          "Choose a color:",
                          Color.WHITE);
```

8.2.6 Load File Dialog

A *file chooser* is a dialog that can be used to navigate to a particular file, either to read from it or to write to it. This section shows example code for reading from a text file.

Necessary imports: javax.swing.JFileChooser, java.io.File, java.io.BufferedReader, java.io.FileReader, and java.io.IOException.

To display a JChooser load file dialog:

```
JFileChooser chooser = new JFileChooser();
chooser.setDialogTitle("Load which file?");
```

To get a reader for the chosen file:

```
BufferedReader br = null;
int result = chooser.showOpenDialog(parent);
if (result == JFileChooser.APPROVE_OPTION) {
  File file = chooser.getSelectedFile();
  try {
    if (file != null) {
      String fileName = file.getCanonicalPath();
      FileReader fr = new FileReader(fileName);
      br = new BufferedReader(fr);
    }
  }
  catch (IOException e) { }
}
```

To read the first line of the file:

```
String line = "";
try { line = br.readLine(); }
catch (IOException e) { }
```

See section 3.3.3 for more ways to read from a file. Close the `FileReader` and `BufferedReader` when you are done.

8.2.7 Save File Dialog

The code for writing to a text file is similar to the code for reading from a text file (see the previous section). You need to use a *save dialog* instead of an *open dialog*, and a `PrintWriter` instead of a `FileReader`.

Necessary imports: `javax.swing.JFileChooser`, `java.io.File`, `java.io.PrintWriter`, `java.io.FileOutputStream`, and `java.io.IOException`.

To display a JChooser save file dialog:

```
JFileChooser chooser = new JFileChooser();
chooser.setDialogTitle("Save file as?");
```

To get the file chosen in a JChooser save file dialog:

```
int result = chooser.showSaveDialog(parent);
PrintWriter pr = null;
if (result == JFileChooser.APPROVE_OPTION) {
    File file = chooser.getSelectedFile();
    String fileName;
    try {
        if (file!= null) {
            fileName = file.getCanonicalPath();
            FileOutputStream stream =
                new FileOutputStream(fileName);
            pr = new PrintWriter(stream, true);
        }
    }
    catch (IOException e) { }
}
```

To write to the file:

```
pr.println("Test line");
pr.close();
```

8.2.8 Custom Dialog

If none of the supplied dialogs is exactly what you need, you can define on your own. What you need to import will depend on what widgets you use; the following code uses javax.swing.JDialog, javax.swing.JFrame, and several components that will be covered later.

To create a JDialog custom dialog:

```
JFrame parent = null;
boolean isModal = true;
JDialog myDialog =
    new JDialog(parent, isModal);
```

To populate a custom dialog just like you would a JPanel:

```
myDialog.add(new JLabel(" Your text "),
        BorderLayout.CENTER);
JButton closeButton = new JButton("Close");
myDialog.add(closeButton, BorderLayout.SOUTH);
```

A custom dialog should have some listeners:

```
closeButton.addActionListener(new ActionListener() {
    public void actionPerformed(ActionEvent e) {
        myDialog.setVisible(false);
    }
});
```

To display the JDialog custom dialog:

```
myDialog.pack();
myDialog.setVisible(true);
```

CHAPTER 9

How to Build a GUI Program

H ERE IS THE GENERAL FORMULA FOR BUILDING a GUI program:

1. Import the necessary packages.

2. Create a window in which to display things—usually a JFrame. Optionally create some JPanels to put in the JFrame.

3. Use the setLayout(*manager*) method to choose a *layout manager* for each JFrame and JPanel. The layout manager is in charge of putting things in the correct places in the window or panel.

4. Create some Components, such as buttons, panels, etc.

5. Ask the layout manager to place the components.

6. Write some Listeners and attach them to your components. When a user interacts with a component, one or more Events will occur, and your Listener can execute some code to handle the event.

7. Display the window.

9.1 EVENT-DRIVEN PROGRAMS

A program without a GUI is in complete control, from beginning to end. It may use some dialogs to interact with the user, but the program is always in control.

A GUI program is different—it is **event-driven**. The program does some initialization, creates the GUI, then waits for something to happen—a mouse click, a key press, a timer signal, the completion of a file transfer, and so on. Each time one of these things occurs, an **event** is created. There may be dozens or even hundreds of events each second, most of which are ignored. The program defines a **listener** for each event it cares about, does something in response to that event, then goes back to "listening" for the next event of interest.

9.2 THE EVENT DISPATCH THREAD

Java programs run in multiple **threads,** (code executing concurrently) and Swing is not **thread safe**—it does not prevent simultaneous access to data, which can result in data corruption. Running a Swing program directly from the main thread can result in rare but unpredictable errors. Unless you are doing parallel programming, all you really need to know is how to run Swing from a special **event dispatch thread**. Here's how:

```
import javax.swing.SwingUtilities;
import javax.swing.JFrame;

public class MyGUI extends JFrame implements Runnable {

    public static void main(String[] args) {
        SwingUtilities.invokeLater(new MyGUI());
    }

    public void run() {
        // add components to this JFrame
        pack();
        setVisible(true);
    }
}
```

The name MyGUI can be changed, but run is a method required by the Runnable interface.

9.3 IMPORT THE NECESSARY PACKAGES

The Swing components are in javax.swing.*, so you always need to import that for a Swing application.

Swing is built on top of AWT and uses a number of AWT packages, including most of the layout managers, so you need to import java.awt.*.

Most listeners also come from the AWT, so you also need to import java.awt.event.*.

A few listeners, such as DocumentListener and ListSelectionListener, are specific to Swing, so if you use them you need to import javax.swing.event.*.

For more complex GUIs, there are additional java.awt.*something* and javax.swing.*something* packages that you may need to import.

> **Note:** The x in javax originally stood for "experimental," but once Swing came into widespread use, it was undesirable to rename the package.

9.4 MAKE A CONTAINER

A *container* is a graphical area that can hold visible components. A *component* is something that can be added to a container.

Two important subclasses of Container are JFrame and JPanel.

For an application, the main (outermost) container is typically a JFrame:

```
JFrame frame = new JFrame(); // or
JFrame frame = new JFrame("Text for title bar");
```

You can create a JFrame in the class that contains the public static void main method, but it's often more convenient to have this class extend JFrame.

A JPanel is both a container (it can have components added to it) and a component (it can be added to containers). Each JPanel has its own layout manager. All but the simplest windows consist of a JFrame containing several JPanels, with each JPanel containing one or more *widgets* (visible GUI components).

To create a JPanel:

```
JPanel panel = new JPanel(); // default: flow layout
JPanel panel = new JPanel(layoutManager);
```

9.5 ADD A LAYOUT MANAGER

Every container (JFrame or JPanel) has a layout manager associated with it. You can use the default layout manager or specify a different one. Here are the layout managers we will cover in some detail:

- BorderLayout (see Figure 9.1) — This is the default layout manager for a JFrame. It provides five areas into which you can put up to five components; any area without a component simply disappears.

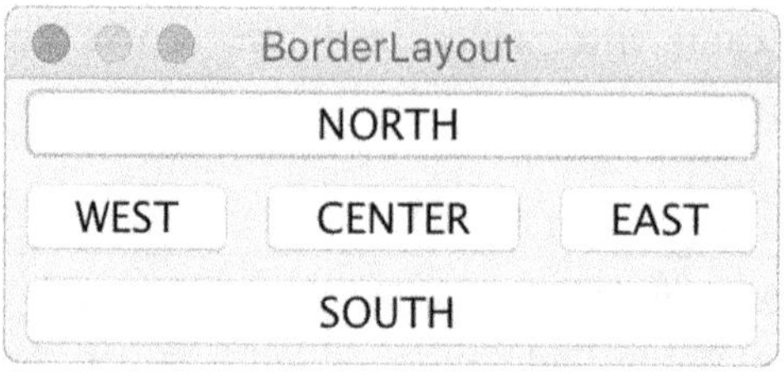

FIGURE 9.1 A BorderLayout.

- FlowLayout (see Figure 9.2) — This is the default layout manager for a JPanel. It just adds components from left to right, top to bottom.

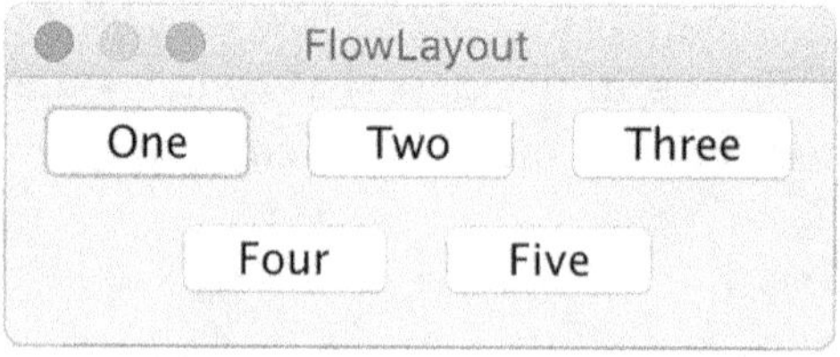

FIGURE 9.2 A FlowLayout.

- GridLayout (see Figure 9.3) — This puts components into a rectangular grid, with all areas being the same size and shape.

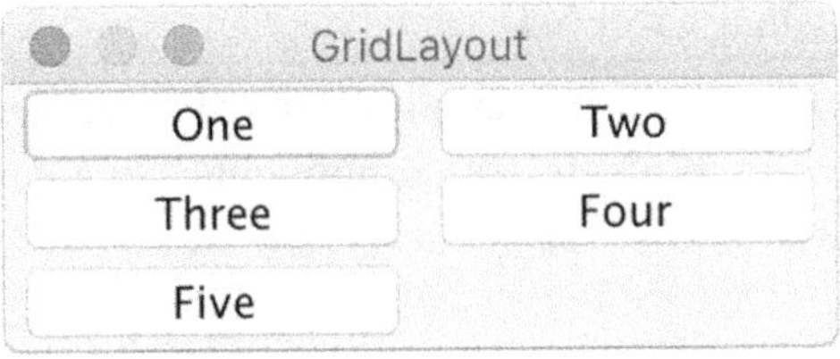

FIGURE 9.3 A GridLayout.

Since there are only a few more kinds of layout managers, they are listed here:

- BoxLayout — Puts components in a single row or single column.

- CardLayout — Uses a JComboBox widget to choose which JPanel to display.

- GridBagLayout — Allows precise control of layout, but is very difficult to use.

- GroupLayout — Works with horizontal and vertical layouts separately.

- SpringLayout — Allows precise control of relationships between components.

To use a layout manager other than the default, call ***container***.setLayout (***layoutManager***). For example:

```
myPanel.setLayout(new GridLayout(rows,columns));
```

Once the layout manager has been determined, components can be added. The method to use depends on the type of layout manager.

- For a flow layout, use ***container***.add(***component***);

- For a grid layout, use either ***container***.add(***component***); or ***container***.add(***component,index***); where the ***index*** is a single integer starting at 0.

- For a border layout, use ***container***.add(***component***, BorderLayout.***area***); where the area is one of NORTH, SOUTH, EAST, WEST, and CENTER. The border areas take up only as much space as necessary to lay out their components, and the center gets all the remaining space.

A JTabbedPane (see section 9.8.4) is not a layout manager but is a good alternative to CardLayout.

9.6 CREATE COMPONENTS

A **widget** is a GUI control, such as a button or text area, intended for the user to interact with. Widgets are components; they can be added to a container such as a JPanel or JFrame.

Figure 9.4 shows some of the more commonly used widgets.

Menu Dialogs Help		
This is a JButton	This is a JTextField	This is a JTextArea; it can have multiple lines
This is a JCheckBox	○ These are JRadioButtons... ...in a ButtonGroup	This is a JLabel
JComboBox	0 10 20 30 40 50	This is a JSpinner 20

FIGURE 9.4   Commonly used widgets.

An **active** widget is one that causes the program to do something whenever it is used. Buttons and most menu items are active: Clicking on an active widget has an immediate effect.

A **passive** widget is one that accepts information but doesn't immediately do something with it; it just holds on to the information until the program asks for it. Text fields, text areas, check boxes, and radio buttons are almost always passive. Some widgets, like combo boxes, can be either active or passive.

A widget is made active by attaching a listener to it.

> **Style rule:** Don't confuse the user by attaching listeners to widgets that are almost always passive.

> **Style rule:** When the user clicks an active widget, it should be obvious that some action has occurred. This can be fairly subtle; for example, many editors display an asterisk next to the file name when a file is modified, and remove the asterisk when the file is saved.

A *tooltip* is a small text message that pops up when the user hovers over a component, usually to give a little more information about the purpose of the component. Tooltips can be added to almost any component.

```
widget.setToolTipText("Purpose of widget");
```

9.7 ADD LISTENERS

Once a GUI program is started up, it typically does nothing more until an *event* occurs. If there is a *listener* for that event, the listener executes some block of code to completion, then nothing more happens until the next event occurs.

Many events are handled "automatically," by built-in listeners. If you type a character while the focus is on a text field, somewhere under the hood there is a listener that responds to the event by drawing that character in the text field. If you click a button, the button "depresses" (changes appearance) as the result of some built-in listener. However, all these built-in listeners do is change the appearance of the text field or button. To have the button do something useful, you must add a listener to it that will execute some code when the button is clicked.

Generally speaking, you shouldn't add listeners to passive widgets like text fields or checkboxes. Instead, just ask for their value when you need to know it.

Different widget types have different kinds of listeners. A JButton should have an ActionListener, while a JSlider might have a ChangeListener.

Some listeners, such as ActionListener, are *functional interfaces*—they define exactly one abstract method. For these listeners, you can simply supply a function, for example,

```
addActionListener(event -> code)
```

Other listeners are not functional interfaces, typically because they specify more than one method. For these, you must define a class that implements all the methods, and provide an object of that class—for example, see the implementation of KeyListener in section 9.8.16.

You can also write listeners for mouse clicks, mouse movement, and key presses, but you don't need to unless you are doing something unusual.

9.8 SAMPLE CODE

Swing is complex. It has many different types of widgets, each of which must be handled slightly differently. The approach taken in this section is to provide a complete sample code for a selection of the more important widgets. In most cases, the code can be adjusted with a few simple tweaks.

When using the widget causes an event to occur, my sample code calls a handleEvent method (not provided) that I wrote for testing purposes. This should be replaced with your code for handling the event.

9.8.1 JFrame and JPanel

The easiest way to create a Swing GUI is to have your main class extend JFrame.

To extend your main class:

```
public class Examples extends JFrame {...}
```

Alternatively, to create a new JFrame:

```
JFrame myFrame = new JFrame();
```

To specify a standard action to take when a JFrame is closed:

```
setDefaultCloseOperation(JFrame.EXIT_ON_CLOSE);
```

or HIDE_ON_CLOSE, DISPOSE_ON_CLOSE, or DO_NOTHING_ON_CLOSE.

To specify a custom action when the JFrame is closed:

```
addWindowListener(new Closer());
private class Closer extends WindowAdapter {
  public void windowClosing(WindowEvent we) {
      update(); // your method
  }
}
```

To make some JPanels to put in the JFrame:

```
JPanel controlPanel = new JPanel();
JPanel outputPanel = new JPanel();
JPanel[] panels = new JPanel[numberOfPanels];
```

To change the layout manager for the JFrame:

```
setLayout(new BorderLayout());
```

To add components to the JFrame (for example, to the NORTH area):

```
add(controlPanel, BorderLayout.NORTH);
```

The last step is usually to cause the JFrame to be sized, laid out, and made visible:

```
pack();
setVisible(true);
```

The above code assumes that it is in a class that extends JFrame. Alternatively, you can create a JFrame and save it in a variable, then send messages to that variable. In particular, the messages setDefaultClose Operation, getContentPane, pack, and setVisible should be sent to the JFrame.

> **Technical note:** It is actually the "content pane" of a JFrame that holds the components; the setLayout and add methods pass these calls along to the content pane. Very old code may still refer to the content pane explicitly.

9.8.2 JEditorPane

An *editor pane* is a special kind of container that supports editing plain text (text/plain) or *hypertext* (text/html). It implements the keyboard shortcuts for cut, copy, and paste, but not undo/redo.

The construction uses somewhat complex nesting. In the example below, the JFrame contains the JScrollPane scroller which contains the JPanel content which contains the JEditorPane editor.

To declare and define a JEditorPane:

```
JEditorPane editor = new JEditorPane();
```

To declare and define a JPanel to serve as the view of a JScrollPane:

```
JPanel content = new JPanel();
```

To declare and define a JScrollPane holding the JPanel:

```
JScrollPane scroller = new JScrollPane(editor);
```

To set the JEditorPane to display HTML:

```
EditorKit kit =
    JEditorPane.createEditorKitForContentType(
        "text/html");
editor.setEditorKit(kit);
```

To add the JEditorPane editor to the content JPanel:

```
content.setLayout(new BorderLayout());
content.add(scroller, BorderLayout.CENTER);
```

By putting the JScrollPane in the CENTER of the JFrame, and not putting anything around the edges, the JScrollPane will fill up the entire JFrame.

To set and get the text of a JEditorPane:

```
editor.setText("This is <i>Sample</i> text");
String myText = editor.getText();
```

9.8.3 JScrollPane

A *scroll pane* can be used to hold any large component that you might want to scroll (in this example, a previously defined JEditorPane named editor).

To declare and define a JPanel to serve as the view of a JScrollPane:

```
JPanel content = new JPanel();
```

To declare and define a JScrollPane holding the JPanel:

```
JScrollPane scroller = new JScrollPane(content);
```

To set the initial size of the JScrollPane:

```
scroller.setPreferredSize(new Dimension(600, 600));
```

To add the JEditorPanel to the JPanel and the JScrollPanel to the JFrame:

```
content.setLayout(new BorderLayout());
content.add(editor, BorderLayout.CENTER);
add(scroller); // to the JFrame
```

To tell the JScrollPane to scroll to a particular character position (by sending a message to the component contained in the JScrollPane):

```
editor.setCaretPosition(0);
```

9.8.4 JTabbedPane

A *tabbed pane* (Figure 9.5) is a container that has tabs like a typical browser window, where clicking each tab reveals different components. It can be used in place of CardLayout.

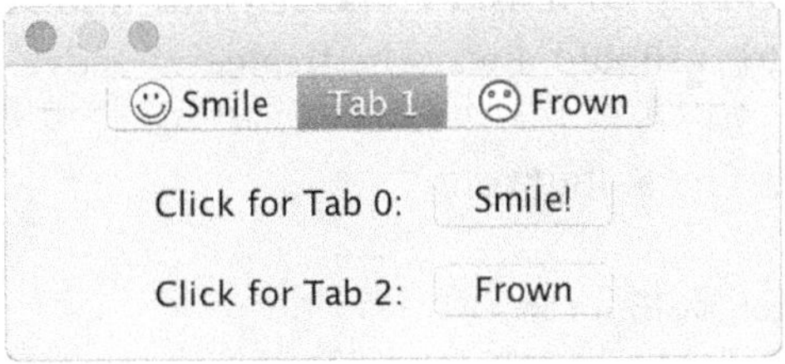

FIGURE 9.5   A JTabbedPane.

To create a tabbed pane and set its size:

```
JTabbedPane tabbedPane = new JTabbedPane();
tabbedPane.setPreferredSize(
  new Dimension(300, 150));
```

To make some icons to put in the tabs:

```
ImageIcon smiley =
  new ImageIcon("Resources Root/smiley.png");
ImageIcon frowny =
  new ImageIcon("Resources Root/frowny.png");
```

To add the tabs, each holding some (previously defined) panel, with optional text, icon, and tooltip.

```
tabbedPane.addTab("Smile", smiley,
                  panel0, "Tooltip 0");
tabbedPane.addTab("Tab 1", null,
                  panel1, "Tooltip 1");
tabbedPane.addTab(null, frowny,
                  panel2, null);
```

To programmatically switch to a tab, use either:

```
tabbedPane.setSelectedIndex(index);
```

or

```
tabbedPane.setSelectedComponent(panel);
```

9.8.5 JButton

A *button* is typically shown as a rectangle with rounded corners, containing text. Buttons should always be treated as active widgets.

To declare and define a JButton:

```
private JButton myJButton =
  new JButton("This is a JButton");
```

To add the JButton to a panel:

```
someJPanel.add(myJButton);
```

To add a listener to the JButton:

```
myJButton.addActionListener(event ->
  handleEvent("JButton"));
```

In this and the following examples, the action being taken is a call to the method handleEvent(*string*). That method call is just a placeholder; it should be replaced with your own code.

9.8.6 JTextField

A *text field* is a rectangle into which a single line of text can be entered. A text field can hold an arbitrary number of characters, although the rectangle may be too small to display them all.

To declare and define a JTextField:

```
private JTextField myJTextField =
    new JTextField("Example JTextField";);
```

To add the JTextField to a panel:

```
someJPanel.add(myJTextField);
```

To add a JToolTip to a JTextField (or any other JComponent):

```
myJTextField.setToolTipText("My tooltip");
```

To set the contents of a JTextField:

```
myJTextField.setText("This is new text");
```

To get the contents of a JTextField:

```
String myText = myJTextField.getText();
```

To add a listener to the JTextField:

```
myJTextField.addActionListener(event ->
    handleEvent("JTextField"));
```

It's usually better to treat a JTextField as a passive widget and use getText() when the value is needed.

9.8.7 JTextArea

A *text area* is a rectangle into which multiple lines of text can be entered. A text area can hold an arbitrary amount of text, although the rectangle may be too small to display all of it. Scroll bars are *not* automatically added to a JTextArea.

To declare and define a JTextArea:

```
private JTextArea myJTextArea =
    new JTextArea(rows, columns);
```

To add the JTextArea to a panel:

```
someJPanel.add(myJTextArea);
```

To set the contents of a JTextArea:

```
myJTextArea.setText(
    "New text for the JTextArea,\n" +
    "and it may contain newlines.");
```

To add to the contents of a JTextArea:

```
myJTextArea.append("Ehh...that's all, folks!");
```

To get the contents of a JTextArea:

```
String myText = myJTextArea.getText();
```

To add a listener to the Document associated with the JTextArea:

```
myJTextArea.getDocument().addDocumentListener(
    new MyJTextAreaListener());
```

To provide the listener (as an inner class) for the JTextArea's Document:

```
public class MyJTextAreaListener
    implements DocumentListener {
    public void insertUpdate(
        DocumentEvent arg0) {
        handleEvent("JTextArea");
    }
    public void removeUpdate(
        DocumentEvent arg0) {
        handleEvent("JTextArea");
    }
```

```
    public void changedUpdate(
      DocumentEvent arg0) {
        handleEvent("JTextArea");
      }
  }
```

Note: You can't attach a listener to the JTextArea itself. Besides, it's usually better to treat a JTextArea as a passive widget and use getText() when the value is needed.

9.8.8 JCheckBox

A *checkbox* is a small square box with an associated label. The box is either checked (has a checkmark in it) or is empty. Each checkbox represents a single yes-no choice and is independent of any other checkboxes.

To declare and define a JCheckBox:

```
private JCheckBox myJCheckBox =
  new JCheckBox("This is a JCheckBox");
```

To add the JCheckBox to a panel:

```
someJPanel.add(myJCheckBox);
```

To find out if a JCheckBox is checked:

```
boolean checked = myJCheckBox.isSelected();
```

To add a listener to the JCheckBox:

```
myJCheckBox.addItemListener(event ->
  handleEvent("JCheckBox"));
```

It's usually better to treat a checkbox as a passive widget and use isSelected() when the value is needed.

9.8.9 JRadioButton

A *radio button* is a small open circle with an associated label. The circle is either selected (filled in) or is empty. Radio buttons are used to select one alternative from among several. Each radio button belongs to a **button group**, so selecting any radio button in the group unselects all the others.

If the program does not specify one particular radio button to be initially selected, then when the program runs, none are selected. Once a selection has been made, it is normally impossible to return to a state where none are selected.

To declare and define some JRadioButtons:

```
private JRadioButton myJRadioButton1 =
    new JRadioButton("radio 1");
private JRadioButton myJRadioButton2 =
    new JRadioButton("radio 2");
```

To declare and define a ButtonGroup to hold the JRadioButtons:

```
private ButtonGroup myButtonGroup = new ButtonGroup();
```

To add the JRadioButtons to a ButtonGroup:

```
myButtonGroup.add(myJRadioButton1);
myButtonGroup.add(myJRadioButton2);
```

To add the JRadioButtons to a panel:

```
someJPanel.setLayout(new GridLayout(2, 1));
someJPanel.add(myJRadioButton1);
someJPanel.add(myJRadioButton2);
```

To initially select some JRadioButton:

```
myJRadioButton1.setSelected(true);
```

To find out which JRadioButton is selected:

```
boolean selected1 = myJRadioButton1.isSelected();
boolean selected2 = myJRadioButton2.isSelected();
```

To add listeners to the JRadioButtons:

```
myJRadioButton1.addItemListener(event ->
  handleEvent("JRadioButton1"));
myJRadioButton2.addItemListener(event ->
  handleEvent("JRadioButton2"));
```

It's usually better to treat radio buttons as passive widgets and use isSelected() when the selected value is needed.

9.8.10 JLabel

Checkboxes and radio buttons have associated labels, but other widgets do not. You can add labels to things, but those labels are normally completely inactive; their only purpose is to provide guidance to the user.

To declare and define a JLabel:

```
JLabel myJLabel = new JLabel("This is a JLabel");
```

To add the JLabel to a panel:

```
labelPanel.add(myJLabel);
```

There is no specific listener for a JLabel. In the unlikely event that you need to listen for mouse clicks on a JLabel, you can add a mouse listener to either the JLabel itself, or to the JPanel that contains the JLabel. Like so:

```
labelPanel.addMouseListener(
  new MouseAdapter() {
    @Override
    public void mouseClicked(
      MouseEvent e) {
        handleEvent("JLabel");
    }
  });
```

9.8.11 JComboBox

To declare and define a JComboBox:

```
private JComboBox myJComboBox =
  new JComboBox(
    new String[]{"Java", "Python",
                 "JavaScript"});
```

To add the JComboBox to a panel:

```
someJPanel.add(myJComboBox);
```

To add a listener to the JComboBox:

```
myJComboBox.addActionListener(event -> {
  String selection =
    (String) myJComboBox.getSelectedItem();
  handleEvent(selection);
});
```

9.8.12 JSlider

A **slider** (Figure 9.6) is a scale that can be manipulated by either the user or the program.

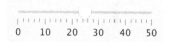

FIGURE 9.6 A JSlider.

To declare and define a JSlider:

```
private JSlider myJSlider =
  new JSlider(SwingConstants.HORIZONTAL,
              0, 50, 20);
```

To add the JSlider to a panel:

```
someJPanel.add(myJSlider);
```

To set some characteristics of the JSlider:

```
myJSlider.setMajorTickSpacing(10);
myJSlider.setMinorTickSpacing(2);
myJSlider.setPaintTicks(true);
myJSlider.setPaintLabels(true);
```

To set the value of a JSlider:

```
myJSlider.setValue(45);
```

To get the value of a JSlider:

```
int temp = myJSlider.getValue();
```

To add a listener to the JSlider:

```
myJSlider.addChangeListener(event ->
  handleEvent("JSlider"));
```

The JSlider can be treated as either an active or a passive widget.

9.8.13 JSpinner

A *spinner* (Figure 9.7) selects a number from a given range of numbers.

FIGURE 9.7   A JSpinner.

To declare and define a numeric JSpinner:

```
int min = 10, max = 30, step = 2, initValue = 20;
SpinnerModel model =
  new SpinnerNumberModel(initValue, min,
                         max, step);
private JSpinner myJSpinner = new JSpinner(model);
```

To add the JSpinner to a panel:

```
someJPanel.add(myJSpinner);
```

To set the value of a JSpinner:

```
myJSpinner.setValue(20);
```

To get the current value of a JSpinner:

```
int value = (int)myJSpinner.getValue();
```

To add a listener to the JSpinner:

```
myJSpinner.addChangeListener(event ->
    handleEvent("JSpinner"));
```

It's usually better to treat a JSpinner as a passive widget and use getValue() when the value is needed. Note that the resultant value must be cast to an int.

9.8.14 JProgressBar

A *progress bar* is a long, thin rectangle that is gradually "filled in" as an operation progresses. When properly set up, it should finish filling at the same time as the operation ends.

To declare and define a numeric JProgressBar:

```
JProgressBar myProgressBar =
    new JProgressBar(min, max);
```

or

```
JProgressBar myProgressBar =
    new JProgressBar(); // 0 to 100
```

To overlay a percent complete message on the progress bar:

```
myProgressBar.setStringPainted(true);
```

To add the JProgressBar to a panel:

```
someJPanel.add(myProgressBar);
```

To set the value of a JProgressBar:

```
myProgressBar.setValue(20);
```

To get the current value of a JProgressBar:

```
int value = myProgressBar.getValue();
```

9.8.15 Menus

The **menu bar** of an application holds **menus**, and each menu holds **menu items** (see Figure 9.8).

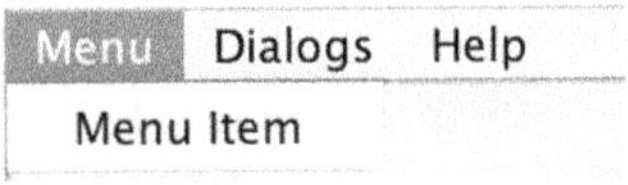

FIGURE 9.8   A JMenuItem in a JMenu.

To declare and define a JMenuBar, a JMenu, and a JMenuItem:

```
JMenuBar myJMenuBar = new JMenuBar();
JMenu myJMenu = new JMenu("Menu");
JMenuItem myJMenuItem = new JMenuItem("Menu Item");
```

To set up the JMenuBar with the JMenu and JMenuItem:

```
myJMenuBar.add(myJMenu);
myJMenu.add(myJMenuItem);
```

To add the JMenuBar (with the JMenu and JMenuItem) to the window:

```
this.setJMenuBar(myJMenuBar);
```

To add a listener to the JMenuItem:

```
myJMenuItem.addActionListener(event ->
    handleEvent("JMenuItem"));
```

9.8.16 Keyboard Input

For typing into text fields, text areas, editor panes, and so on, all the user's key presses are handled automatically; the programmer doesn't have to do anything. For other uses, you may wish to add a KeyListener to a Container of your choice.

To do some routine setup:

```
JPanel panel = new JPanel();
panel.setPreferredSize(new Dimension(300, 200));
JLabel label = new JLabel("Type here");
panel.add(label);
add(panel, BorderLayout.CENTER); // to JFrame
```

To define a KeyListener and attach it to a JPanel:

```
KeyListener listener = new KeyListener() {
  @Override
  public void keyPressed(KeyEvent e) {
    System.out.println(
      "Pressed " + e.getKeyCode());
  }
  @Override
  public void keyTyped(KeyEvent e) {
    System.out.println(
      "Typed:" + e.getKeyChar());
  }
  @Override
  public void keyReleased(KeyEvent e) {
    System.out.println(
      " Released: " + e.getKeyCode());
  }
};
panel.setFocusable(true);
panel.addKeyListener(listener);
```

Notes:

- When a character is typed, the event handlers keyPressed, keyTyped, and keyReleased are called, in that order. When other keys (shift, option, up arrow, etc.) are typed, only keyPressed and keyReleased are called.

- All three methods can use getKeyCode(), which returns an int.

- The keyTyped method (only) can use the getKeyChar method to return the char.

- A Container must have "focus" in order to respond to events. Usually, this occurs by clicking on it or tabbing to it.

- To determine which key was pressed, you can compare the **key code** to any of a large number of constants in the KeyEvent class, such as VK_A, VK_SHIFT, or VJ_DOWN. Non-English keyboards have the keys arranged differently, but the VK (virtual keyboard) values are independent of the keyboard arrangement.

9.8.17 Mouse Input

All of the common widgets handle mouse events automatically. However, if you wish to do something special, such as point at specific parts of an image, you can write your own mouse listeners. There are separate listeners for clicks, movement, and scrolling.

The MouseListener interface specifies five public void methods: mouseEntered, mouseExited, mousePressed, mouseReleased, and mouseClicked. Each of these receives a MouseEvent argument (see below). The only one of these methods you are likely to care about is mouseClicked, but MouseListener is an interface, so you have to provide them all, even if they don't do anything.

The MouseMotionListener interface specifies two public void methods, mouseMoved and mouseDragged, both with a MouseEvent argument.

The MouseEvent object has the following methods (among others):

- getButton() returns one of the values MouseEvent.BUTTON1, MouseEvent.BUTTON2, or MouseEvent.BUTTON3.

- getX() and getY() return the mouse location, in pixels, relative to the top-left corner of the component that has the listener. X values increase as the mouse pointer moves to the right, and Y values increase as the mouse pointer moves down.

- getXOnScreen() and getYOnScreen() return the mouse location relative to the top-left corner of the display screen.

- getClickCount() returns the number of closely-spaced mouse clicks.

The MouseAdapter class provides empty versions of all of the above methods, so you can extend this class and override any of the methods you care to use. See section 9.8.10 on the JLabel widget for an example of using a MouseAdapter.

There is also a MouseWheelListener interface. It requires a mouseWheelMoved method with a MouseWheelEvent parameter. Since a JScrollPane is almost always more convenient, this interface is not covered here.

9.9 DICEROLLER

Here is a complete (but very small) Swing application:

```
import javax.swing.*;
import javax.swing.event.*;
import java.awt.*;
import java.awt.event.*;
import java.util.Random;

public class DiceRoller extends JFrame {
    static Random rand = new Random();
    JButton rollButton;
    JTextField result;

    public static void main(String[] args) {
        SwingUtilities.invokeLater(new Runnable() {
            public void run() {
                new DiceRoller().createAndShowGUI();
            }
        });
    }

    void createAndShowGUI() {
        setDefaultCloseOperation(JFrame.EXIT_ON_CLOSE);
```

```
rollButton = new JButton("Roll 'em!");
getContentPane().add(rollButton, BorderLayout.NORTH);
result = new JTextField("You haven't rolled yet.");
getContentPane().add(result, BorderLayout.SOUTH);
pack();
setVisible(true);
rollButton.addActionListener(event -> {
        int number = rand.nextInt(6) + 1;
        result.setText("You rolled a " + number);
    });
}
}
```

CHAPTER 10

Threads and Animation

U SEFUL CLASSES THAT HAVE BEEN DESCRIBED in varying levels of detail are StringBuilder, Scanner, Stack, and HashMap. This section describes some additional classes and methods that are important for writing concurrent programs and for doing animation.

Every one of these classes is far richer than this section would suggest. Only the basics are described here.

10.1 THREADS

A *thread* is the flow of control in a program. Modern operating systems are *multiprocessing:* they do many things at the same time. This might be accomplished by assigning different threads to different cores, or by interrupting one thread to turn over execution to another. Even a simple Java program uses multiple threads and hides the details so you don't have to think about them. You can, however, directly create and manipulate threads.

A Thread is an object representing a flow of control. When you step through a program, you are following a thread. Threads are just like any other object; you can create them and send messages to them. Every program uses threads.

There are two ways to create another Thread and start it running:

- Write a class that extends Thread and overrides the public void run() method.

  - Create an object of this class.

  - Send the object the (inherited) start() message.

- Write a class that implements Runnable and overrides the public void run() method.

  - Create an object *obj* of this class.

  - Create a new Thread(*obj*).

  - Send the Thread the start() message.

A Thread can be in one of four states (see Figure 10.1):

- **Ready:** all set to run

- **Running:** actually doing something

- **Waiting**, or **blocked:** needs something

- **Dead:** will never do anything again

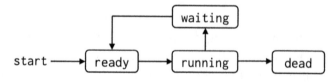

FIGURE 10.1   States of a thread.

Execution is controlled by the Java scheduler, but you can request it to do some things. A call to start() is one such request. Another is that you can request the current Thread to pause for a given number of milliseconds.

Thread.sleep(*milliseconds*);

It is possible for this call to raise an InterruptedException.

```
try {Thread.sleep(1000);}
catch (InterruptedException e) { }
```

Warning: The very first version of Java allowed one Thread to control other Threads with the methods stop, suspend, and resume. This was immediately recognized as a Bad Idea, and those methods were immediately deprecated. Never use them!

A simple alternative to using deprecated methods is for one thread to set a flag that can be read by another thread.

```
boolean okToRun = true;
secondThread.start();

public void run() {
    while (firstThread.okToRun) {...}
}
```

10.2 SYNCHRONIZATION

There are many cases when it is desirable to have many processes (threads) running in parallel. For example, other work could be done while a slow database access or file transfer is in process.

Subtle, irreproducible errors can result when a value is being changed by one thread while being accessed by a different thread, or when two threads both try to update the same value. To avoid this situation, Java introduces the concept of *synchronization*, which simply means giving one thread temporary but exclusive access to a value or set of values.

You can synchronize on an object:

```
synchronized (obj) { code }
```

Here, synchronized is being used as a statement. No other code can synchronize on object *obj* until the *code* finishes.

Note 1: It often makes sense to synchronize on the object you want to access or modify, but this is not a requirement. Any object can be used for synchronization, and the *code* might access or modify completely unrelated values.

Note 2: Synchronizing on an object prevents *only* other threads synchronizing on the *same* object from running. Unsynchronized code, or code synchronizing on other objects, is not affected.

You can synchronize a method:

```
synchronized void methodName(arguments) { code }
```

In this case, `synchronized` is being used as a method modifier; it synchronizes on the object `this`.

Synchronizing on an object means that the thread gets a "lock" on that object, and no other thread can synchronize on it until the code finishes and the lock is released. While it has the lock, the thread can also use any other methods that synchronize on the same object. Again, there is no protection from unsynchronized code, or from code that synchronizes on some other object.

The point of multithreading is to allow different threads to run at the same time, so long as they are not attempting to access the same objects. Synchronization is expensive, and it is very difficult to maintain correctness while pursuing efficiency.

10.3 TIMERS

A `javax.swing.Timer` is used to schedule code for repeated execution. The constructor takes two parameters: an `int` time in milliseconds, which is used to set both the initial delay and the time between events; and an `ActionListener` (usually an anonymous inner class) to do something at each "tick" of the `Timer`.

```
Timer timer = new Timer(40, event -> doSomething());
```

There are a number of messages that can be sent to a Timer, including `stop()`, `start()`, `setDelay(ms)`, and `restart()`.

10.4 PROPERTY CHANGES

A `java.beans.PropertyChangeSupport` object is one way that an object can inform other objects that it has been updated.

Terminology: A *bean* is any Java class that (1) has a no-argument constructor, (2) has at least some "properties" (private fields) that have getters and setters, and (3) is serializable. Saying that a class is a bean is simply saying that it has these characteristics.

Basic operation is as follows:

1. Create a new `PropertySupportObject(`*bean*`)`, where *bean* is the object to be "watched" or "listened to."

2. Each time the bean completes an update, it should send the message `firePropertyChange(`*propertyName*`,`*oldValue*`,`*newValue*`)` to the `PropertySupportObject`. This is probably best done within the bean itself.

   - The *propertyName* is a String, and the *oldValue* and *newValue* can be the values of the entire *bean* object, or of some part of it.

   - This method will only cause a `PropertyChangeEvent` to occur if the *oldValue* and the *newValue* are different.

3. To add a listener to the bean, send the message add `PropertyChangeListener(`*listener*`)` to the `PropertySupportObject`. Any number of listeners may be added.

4. To listen to a bean, a class must implement `Property ChangeListener` and override the inherited `public void propertyChange(PropertyChangeEvent `*event*`)` method.

   - The *event* parameter has the accessible fields *event*`.propertyName`, *event*`.oldValue`, and *event*`.newValue`. The latter two are of type `Object`, so should be cast to the desired type.

It isn't necessary for a class to have all the bean characteristics in order to use the above classes and methods.

10.5 SwingWorker

A *worker thread* provides a means of running a long-running process on a background thread so that the main thread can continue to do work. This is particularly important in a GUI (graphical user interface) program, where a long-running process can make the GUI unresponsive.

The SwingWorker class provides a simple way to create a worker thread. There are three threads involved:

- The **current thread** creates and starts a SwingWorker, then continues to run without interruption.

- The **worker thread** executes the long-running code.

- The **event dispatch** thread handles all the GUI events.

To begin, create a class (for example, Worker) that extends SwingWorker with two type parameters *T* and *V*, where *T* is the type of value to be computed by the worker thread and *V* is a type that can be sent to the GUI.

To keep the example short, we will not use a GUI. The long-running process typically is some file or database manipulation, but for our example, we will try to find one factor of a big integer.

```java
import java.math.BigInteger;
import javax.swing.SwingWorker;

class Worker extends SwingWorker<BigInteger, Void> {
  private BigInteger big;

  Worker(BigInteger big) { // constructor
    this.big = big;
  }

  @Override
  public BigInteger doInBackground() {
    return findFactor(big);
  }

  // Here is our long-running process
  BigInteger findFactor(BigInteger big) {
    if (big.mod(BigInteger.TWO).equals
      (BigInteger.ZERO)) {
      return BigInteger.TWO; // 2 is a factor
    }

    BigInteger divisor = new BigInteger("3");
    while (big.divide(divisor).compareTo(divisor) >= 0) {
```

```
         if (big.mod(divisor).equals(BigInteger.ZERO)) {
            return divisor;
         }
         divisor = divisor.add(BigInteger.TWO);
      }
      return BigInteger.ZERO;
   }
}
```

In the class header *T*, the type of value to compute, is a BigInteger, while *V* is unused.

The class has a constructor which accepts and stores the data it is to use—in this case, a BigInteger to try to factor. It has one necessary method, *T* doInBackground().

The doInBackground method could contain the long-running code, but we have put that in a separate method, findFactor, called from doInBackground. The findFactor method tries to find and return one factor of a BigInteger, big, but it will return zero if big is prime. We have not previously discussed the BigInteger class, but its methods (add, divide, etc.) are mostly self-explanatory.

The main class, FactorFinder, uses Worker.

```
import java.math.BigInteger;

public class FactorFinder {

   public static void main(String[] args) {
      new FactorFinder(args[0]);
   }

   public FactorFinder(String bignum) {
      BigInteger factor = BigInteger.ZERO;
      BigInteger big = new BigInteger(bignum);
      System.out.println("Trying to factor " + big);

      // Use the SwingWorker
      Worker worker = new Worker(big);
      worker.execute();
      while (!worker.isDone()) {
```

```
        twiddleThumbs();
    }
    try { factor = worker.get(); }
    catch (Exception e) { }

    // Show the results
    if (factor.equals(BigInteger.ZERO))
        System.out.println("\n" + big +
                            " is prime");
    else
        System.out.println("\n" + big + " = " +
                            factor +" x " +
                            big.divide(factor));
}

public void twiddleThumbs() {
    try { Thread.sleep(1000); }
    catch(InterruptedException e) {}
    System.out.print('.');
}
}
```

The main method gets a number, as a String, from the command line (or from a setting in the IDE). It makes a BigInteger from the string, creates a Worker object with this BigInteger, and tells the Worker object to execute().

Note: A good number to try is "41758540882408627201."

Once a second, twiddleThumbs method asks the worker object if it isDone(), and if not, it prints out a period. The only purpose of this is to show that the current thread continues uninterrupted. In a GUI, we might instead update a progress bar.

Eventually, the get() method returns a result. If called before the worker thread is finished, the current thread stops and waits for it to finish; this isn't what is generally desired. The get() method could throw an InterruptedException or an ExecutionException, so get() is put in a try-catch statement to handle these.

Finally, the result is printed.

10.6 THE BOUNCING BALL

Animation is performed by displaying a series of still images, one after the other, with minor changes between each image and the next. A bouncing ball is the "Hello world" of animation—a small disk that moves steadily across a window, and "bounces" (changes direction) when it encounters an edge of the window. Our version (see Figure 10.2) will have two buttons, **Run** to start the animation and **Stop** to pause it.

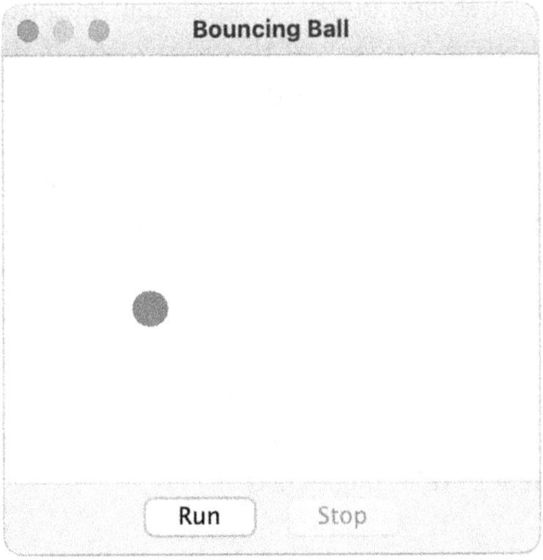

FIGURE 10.2   The Bouncing Ball example.

Our implementation uses the MVC model, with the unimaginatively named classes Model, View, and Controller. The controller sets up the GUI and creates objects of the other two types; the model controls the position of the ball; and the view displays the ball in the window.

The model is treated as a "bean" (although it does not have all the characteristics of a bean), and PropertyChangeEvents are used to keep the model as independent as possible from the rest of the code.

In the following we mention only the main points of the Bouncing Ball program; the complete code is in an appendix.

10.6.1 MVC

MVC, or *Model-View-Controller* is a useful design pattern when one thread is used to control another thread, such as when doing animation.

> **Terminology:** A *design pattern* is simply a way of organizing code that has been found to be generally useful. MVC is considered here in order to introduce some useful objects and interfaces.

The *model* is the code doing the actual work of the simulation, animation, or whatever. It should be free of any input/output, and completely independent of both the view and the controller. If there is a GUI, it should be completely unknown to the model.

The *view* displays information about what is going on in the model. In the case of an animation, it displays the current frame of the animation.

The *controller* is used to send commands or information to the model.

The model, view, and controller can be implemented as three separate classes, but in small GUI programs, it is often convenient to combine the controller and view into a single class.

10.6.2 Controller

The controller's main job is to set up the GUI, so it extends JFrame and adds **Run** and **Stop** buttons. It creates the model and the view. Since the view has to know about the model, but the model doesn't have to know about the view, the model is created first.

```
model = new Model();
view = new View(model);
```

Since the ball is to bounce off the edges of the window, it has to know where those are. The top and left edges are at 0; the right edge is the width of the window, and the bottom edge is the height of the window. If the window is resized, the new values must be fetched and sent to the model.

```
this.addComponentListener(new ComponentAdapter() {
    @Override
```

```
public void componentResized(ComponentEvent e) {
  model.setLimits(view.getWidth(),
                  view.getHeight());
}
});
```

10.6.3 Model

The model has four basic variables: the x and y position of the ball, and the amount that each of these changes from one frame (still picture) to the next. For convenience in drawing the ball, the x and y coordinates are given as the top left corner of a square enclosing the ball. For convenience in creating a single object for the viewer to see, the x and y are enclosed in a Point object.

```
private Point position = new Point(0, 0);
private int dx = 6; // change in x
private int dy = 4; // change in y
```

The model uses a Timer to add dx to x and dy to y at 40-millisecond intervals, or 25 times a second. This is sufficient to give the illusion of motion.

```
timer = new Timer(40, new ActionListener() {
  @Override
  public void actionPerformed(ActionEvent e) {
    makeOneStep();
  }
});
```

At each step, the x position is advanced by dx, and the y position by dy. A "bounce" occurs when the ball goes too far to the left or too far to the right, and this is accomplished by changing the sign of dx.

```
position.x += dx;
if (position.x < 0 || position.x >= xLimit) {
  dx = -dx;
  position.x += dx;
}
```

The code for updating position.y is almost identical.

The model represents a ball bouncing around within a bounding box. It is irrelevant to the model that the bounding box corresponds to the edges of a window. It is perfectly legal to draw outside a window; anything drawn there simply isn't visible.

To make the new position available to other classes, the model has a PropertyChangeSupport object (named pcs). This is public so that it can be accessed by the view class.

```
public PropertyChangeSupport pcs;
```

Each time the model completes a step, it tells pcs to fire off an event containing the new value of the ball's position.

```
this.pcs.firePropertyChange("position", null,
                            position);
```

10.6.4 View

The task of the view class is simply to clear the window and draw a ball in it each time it receives a PropertyChangeEvent. This means it has to "listen" for those events. To do this, it implements PropertyChangeListener.

```
public class View extends JPanel
    implements PropertyChangeListener {…}
```

It has to provide a listener for the events:

```
@Override
public void propertyChange(
    PropertyChangeEvent event) {
  position = (Point) event.getNewValue();
  repaint();
}
```

But this isn't enough; one more step is required: The View class is now a listener, but the same PropertyChangeSupport object used earlier must be told about it.

```
model.pcs.addPropertyChangeListener(this);
```

You can think of the View as "subscribing" to the series of events sent out by pcs.

Appendix A:
Code for BouncingBall

```java
/**
 * This is an example of the basic "Bouncing
 * Ball" animation, making use of the Model-
 * View-Controller design pattern and the
 * Timer and PropertyChangeSupport classes.
 */

import java.awt.BorderLayout;
import java.awt.event.ActionEvent;
import java.awt.event.ActionListener;
import java.awt.event.ComponentAdapter;
import java.awt.event.ComponentEvent;
import java.util.Timer;
import javax.swing.JButton;
import javax.swing.JFrame;
import javax.swing.JPanel;

/**
 * The Controller sets up the GUI and handles
 * the controls (in this case, buttons).
 * @author David Matuszek
 */
```

```java
public class Controller extends JFrame {
  JPanel buttonPanel = new JPanel();
  JButton runButton = new JButton("Run");
  JButton stopButton = new JButton("Stop");
  Timer timer;

  /**
   * The Model is the object that does all
   * the computations. It is independent
   * of the Controller and View objects.
   */
  Model model;

  /**
   * The View object displays what is
   * happening in the Model.
   */
  View view;

  /**
   * Runs the bouncing ball program.
   * @param args Ignored.
   */
  public static void main(String[] args) {
    Controller c = new Controller();
    c.init();
    c.display();
  }

  /**
   * Sets up communication between the
   * Model and the View.
   */
  private void init() {
    model = new Model();
    view = new View(model);
  }

  /**
   * Displays the GUI.
   */
  private void display() {
    layOutComponents();
```

```
    attachListenersToComponents();
    setSize(300, 300);
    setVisible(true);
    setDefaultCloseOperation(
      JFrame.EXIT_ON_CLOSE);
  }
/**
 * Arranges the components in the GUI.
 */
  private void layOutComponents() {
    setLayout(new BorderLayout());
    this.add(BorderLayout.SOUTH, buttonPanel);
    buttonPanel.add(runButton);
    buttonPanel.add(stopButton);
    stopButton.setEnabled(false);
    this.add(BorderLayout.CENTER, view);
  }

/**
 * Attaches listeners to the components
 * and schedules a Timer.
 */
  private void attachListenersToComponents() {
      // The Run button starts the Model
    runButton.addActionListener( event -> {
      runButton.setEnabled(false);
      stopButton.setEnabled(true);
      model.start();
    });
      // The Stop button pauses the Model
    stopButton.addActionListener(event -> {
      runButton.setEnabled(true);
      stopButton.setEnabled(false);
      model.pause();
    });
      // When the window is resized,
      // the Model is given the new limits
    this.addComponentListener(
          new ComponentAdapter() {
      @Override
      public void componentResized(
          ComponentEvent arg0) {
```

```
      model.setLimits(view.getWidth(),
                      view.getHeight());
      }
    });
  }
}
```

BOUNCING BALL: MODEL

```java
import java.awt.event.ActionEvent;
import java.awt.event.ActionListener;
import java.awt.Point;
import javax.swing.Timer;
import java.beans.*;

/**
 * This is the Model class for a bouncing ball.
 * It defines a PropertyChangeSupport object.
 * @author David Matuszek
 */
public class Model {
   private Point position = new Point(0, 0);
   private int xLimit, yLimit;
   private int dx = 6;
   private int dy = 4;
   private Timer timer;
   public PropertyChangeSupport pcs;

   public Model() {
     pcs = new PropertyChangeSupport(this);
     position = new Point(0, 0);
     timer = new Timer(
         40, new ActionListener() {
     @Override
     public void actionPerformed(
         ActionEvent e) {
           makeOneStep();
         }
     });
     timer.stop();
   }
```

```java
/**
 * Sets the "walls" that the ball should
 * bounce off from.
 * @param xLimit The right wall (in pixels).
 * @param yLimit The floor (in pixels).
 */
public void setLimits(int xLimit,
                        int yLimit) {
   this.xLimit = xLimit - 20;
   this.yLimit = yLimit - 20;
   position =
     new Point(Math.min(position.x, xLimit),
               Math.min(position.y, yLimit));
}

/**
 * @return The balls X position.
 */
public Point getPosition() {
   return position;
}

/**
 * Tells the ball to start moving. This is
 * done by starting a Timer that periodically
 * tells the ball to make one "step."
 */
public void start() {
   timer.start();
}

/**
 * Tells the ball to stop where it is.
 */
public void pause() {
   timer.stop();
}

/**
 * Tells the ball to advance one step
 * in the direction that it is moving.
 * If it hits a wall, its direction
 * of movement changes. The method
```

```
 * then fires a PropertyChange event.
 */
public void makeOneStep() {
   // Do the work
   position.x += dx;
   if (position.x < 0 ||
       position.x >= xLimit) {
     dx = -dx;
     position.x += dx;
   }
   position.y += dy;
   if (position.y < 0 ||
       position.y >= yLimit) {
     dy = -dy;
     position.y += dy;
   }
   this.pcs.firePropertyChange(
       "position", null, position);
 }
}
```

BOUNCING BALL: VIEW

```
import java.awt.Color;
import java.awt.Graphics;
import java.awt.Point;
import java.beans.*;
import javax.swing.JPanel;

/**
 * The View displays what is going on in
 * the Model. In this example, the Model
 * is only a single bouncing ball.
 * @author David Matuszek
 */
public class View extends JPanel
    implements PropertyChangeListener {
Point position = new Point(0, 0);
/** This is what we will be viewing. */
Model model;
```

```java
/**
 * Constructor. Adds a listener for
 * PropertyChange events.
 * @param model The Model whose working
 *       is to be displayed.
 */
View(Model model) {
   this.model = model;
   model.pcs.addPropertyChangeListener(this);
 }

/**
 * Displays what is going on in the Model.
 * Note: This method should NEVER be
 * called directly; call repaint() instead.
 * @param g The Graphics on which to paint.
 * @see javax.swing.JComponent#paint(
 * java.awt.Graphics)
 */
@Override
public void paint(Graphics g) {
   g.setColor(Color.WHITE);
   g.fillRect(0, 0, getWidth(), getHeight());
   g.setColor(Color.RED);
   position = model.getPosition();
   g.fillOval(position.x, position.y, 20, 20);
 }

/**
 * Repaints the JPanel when a
 * PropertyChangeEvents is received.
 * @param evt Contains the ball's position.
 */
@Override
public void propertyChange(
     PropertyChangeEvent evt) {
   position = (Point) evt.getNewValue();
   repaint();
 }
}
```

Index

Note to editor: To help you distinguish the computer font (Inconsolata) from the text font, I have made the computer font larger and blue. Notice in particular that all the symbols in the first group (from ! to ~) should be in the computer font. For the edited index, the color should be removed and the same font size used throughout.

Note: Page numbers in **bold** indicate defined terms.

Printed in the USA
CPSIA information can be obtained
at www.ICGtesting.com
LVHW010935190324
774517LV00003BA/275